Building a Sustainable Political Economy: SPERI Research & Policy

Series Editors

Colin Hay
University of Sheffield
Department of Politics
Sheffield, UK

Anthony Payne
University of Sheffield
Department of Politics
Sheffield, UK

Aims of the Series

The Sheffield Political Economy Research Institute (SPERI) is an innovation in higher education research and outreach. It brings together leading international researchers in the social sciences, policy makers, journalists and opinion formers to reassess and develop proposals in response to the political and economic issues posed by the current combination of financial crisis, shifting economic power and environmental threat. Building a Sustainable Political Economy: SPERI Research & Policy will serve as a key outlet for SPERI's published work. Each title will summarise and disseminate to an academic and postgraduate student audience, as well as directly to policy-makers and journalists, key policy-oriented research findings designed to further the development of a more sustainable future for the national, regional and world economy following the global financial crisis. It takes a holistic and interdisciplinary view of political economy in which the local, national, regional and global interact at all times and in complex ways. The SPERI research agenda, and hence the focus of the series, seeks to explore the core economic and political questions that require us to develop a new sustainable model of political economy.t at all times and in complex ways. The SPERI research agenda, and hence the focus of the series, seeks to explore the core economic and political questions that require us to develop a new sustainable model of political economy.

More information about this series at
http://www.springer.com/mycopy/series/[14879]

Craig Berry

Austerity Politics and UK Economic Policy

Craig Berry
Sheffield Political Economy Research Institute
Sheffield, UK

Building a Sustainable Political Economy: SPERI Research & Policy
ISBN 978-1-137-59009-1   ISBN 978-1-137-59010-7 (eBook)
DOI 10.1057/978-1-137-59010-7

Library of Congress Control Number: 2016939233

Printed on acid-free paper

This Palgrave Macmillan imprint is published by Springer Nature
The registered company is Macmillan Publishers Ltd. London

For The Dream Team

Acknowledgements

This book is a product of my research since 2013 on the transformation of the British growth model, but also, in a very important sense, a collective effort of the Sheffield Political Economy Research Institute (SPERI), where I am based as Deputy Director. I am hugely grateful to SPERI's directors Tony Payne and Colin Hay for the opportunity to have conducted this research, and to Tony especially for creating such a vibrant and supportive environment, in both personal and intellectual terms, within which to work.

Everybody that has been connected to SPERI over the past few years has helped me in one way or another. In addition to Tony and Colin, I am particularly grateful for the support and friendship of Sarah Boswell, Laure Astill, Tom Hunt, Hannah Lambie-Mumford, Martin Craig, Scott Lavery, Adam Barber, Jeremy Green, Genevieve LeBaron, and Tom Hastings. Colin and Scott deserve special thanks as collaborators on parts of the research that underpins the book's analysis, and I am very grateful also for the encouraging and constructive feedback from an anonymous reviewer. Many others based elsewhere have played an important role too, especially but not exclusively Daniel Bailey, Richard Exell, Matthew Watson, Martin Jones, Arianna Giovannini, Rachel Reeves, Martin McIvor, Richard Berry, and Colin Wray, and Amber Husain and Christina Brian at Palgrave.

The book is dedicated to my wife Laura and our daughters Miriam and Sylvia. My children, who came along in March 2013 and January 2015, have enriched my life more than I could possibly have imagined. They inspire me in every single moment in ways they cannot yet appreciate, and I can only promise now to tell them how grateful I am once they can.

My debt to Laura is no less significant, but I fear it is one I cannot possibly service. She is a wonderful mother, a formidable sounding board, and my best friend. Nothing I do is conceivable without Laura, and I hope she knows how much I adore her, and how profoundly and eternally grateful I am. Last but not least, I need also to thank my parents and Laura's parents for all their love and kindness.

Contents

Abbreviations

ALMP	Active labour market policy
BBC	British Broadcasting Corporation
BIS	Department for Business, Innovation and Skills
CPI	Consumer Price Index
CRESC	Centre for Research on Socio-Cultural Change
CTF	Child Trust Fund
DWP	Department for Work and Pensions
ECB	European Central Bank
EU	European Union
FLS	Funding for Lending Scheme
FND	Flexible New Deal
GDP	Gross domestic product
GIB	Green Investment Bank
GVA	Gross value added
HTB	Help to Buy
HTW	Help to Work
IMF	International Monetary Fund
JCP	Jobcentre Plus
JSA	Jobseeker's Allowance
LEP	Local Enterprise Partnership
MP	Member of Parliament
MPC	Monetary Policy Committee
MWA	Mandatory Work Activity
NHS	National Health Service
OBR	Office for Budget Responsibility
OECD	Organisation for Economic Co-operation and Development
ONS	Office for National Statistics

PQE	People's quantitative easing
QE	Quantitative easing
SG	Saving Gateway
SMEs	Small- and medium-sized enterprises
SNP	Scottish National Party
SPERI	Sheffield Political Economy Research Institute
UC	Universal Credit
UKIP	UK Independence Party
VAT	Value added tax
WAS	Wealth and Assets Survey

CHAPTER 1

Introduction: Austerity and Growth

Abstract 'Growth model' is an analytical concept which designates the main sources of economic growth within a given economy, the orientation of institutions configured to enable the associated economic activities, and, crucially, patterns of wealth distribution which sustain certain economic and political practices. The 'neoliberal' or 'Anglo-liberal' growth model evident in the UK before the financial crisis built upon longstanding traditions within the UK economy and economic policy practice, such as the centrality of the finance sector, fiscal conservatism, international openness, low taxation, and limited employment protection. UK policy elites have acted to rescue this model since the 2008 crisis, and the 'austerity' agenda pursued by the coalition and Conservative governments since 2010 has served to reinforce many of its intellectual, behavioural, and distributional foundations.

Keywords Growth • Austerity • Financial crisis • Neoliberalism • Ideas

That the UK economy needed to change in the wake of the 2008 financial crisis is something that most of the policymaking community (especially, it seems, elected politicians) and academic commentators (especially, as you would expect, critical political economists) were virtually unanimous on.

C. Berry, *Austerity Politics and UK Economic Policy*, Building a Sustainable Political Economy: SPERI Research & Policy,
DOI 10.1057/978-1-137-59010-7_1

We now know that, in practice, any change that has occurred has been relatively superficial. Even in the one area of economic practice in which policymaking elites have apparently been prepared to instigate radical change—public expenditure—the rhetoric has often failed to match the reality. As such, we are repeatedly told that a severe reduction in public spending and borrowing is necessary, but that the most significant cuts will occur in the near (or not so near) future. This is not to downplay the significance and impact of cuts in spending (notably local government) or entitlements (i.e., social security benefits) in some areas, but rather to suggest that what is most significant about the elite agenda on fiscal policy is not what it actually entails, but the narrative employed to justify what it might entail.

The central concept of this narrative has of course been 'austerity', a concept that has been so successful in attaining the status of common sense within post-crisis political discourse that its advocates rarely use the term itself anymore. Policymakers understand that few members of the electorate relish the implications of the apparent austerity agenda, yet also that the public accepts its necessity almost unthinkingly. But given that the thing deemed necessary amounts to something quite different to what is commonly understood as austerity, this book argues that the most important implication of austerity is its success in generating the *illusion* of change in fiscal management, and shielding from scrutiny the considerable effort by policymakers to actually *prevent* change in the way that the UK economy operates. The book develops this argument by offering an analysis of several key areas of UK economic policy and associated political processes, since the establishment of the coalition government in 2010. This introductory chapter outlines the analytical context of the book's content by exploring the relationship between economic growth and economic policy, and then briefly discusses the political and ideological context from which the austerity agenda has emerged.

Growth and Growth Models

The theoretical basis of the book's analysis is that the UK political economy is characterised by a discernible 'growth model', defined as the main sources of economic growth within the economy—insofar as they are distinguishable from other capitalist economies—and the orientation of political and economic institutions configured to enable the associated economic activities. In positing a co-dependent and mutually constitutive relationship between the political and economic spheres, the growth model concept is inherently associated with political economy as a form of analysis, and it is thus acknowledged here that its value rests upon the perceived efficacy of political economy in general. Such contestability is unavoidable. It should also be acknowledged that there are other approaches, broadly situated within political economy, that offer similar but alternative conceptualisations. The most obvious examples are the notion of a 'regime of accumulation', associated with the Marxist regulation school (Jessop 1990), and the notion of 'varieties of capitalism', associated with institutionalist political economy (Hall and Soskice 2001). To simplify enormously, the former places more ontological weight on capitalist production processes (while seeking to understand how institutions 'regularise' these processes), and the latter emphasises the role of political institutions in determining an economy's dominant activities. The growth model concept might be conceived as falling somewhere between these two approaches; indeed, it is assumed here to be broad enough to encapsulate both. This book also contends that all of the approaches discussed here are guilty, to some extent, of underemphasising the ideational realm of political economy (Berry 2011); the greater flexibility, in ontological terms, of the notion of a growth model makes it an exception, albeit, judged by the research conducted through this lens to date, only a partial one.

The growth model evident in the UK political economy in the period immediately before the financial crisis built upon long standing traditions within the UK economy and economic policy practice, while incorporating some novel elements related, essentially, to the management of post-industrial decline in many provincial regions. The economic importance of the finance industry, traditionally the 'cuckoo in the nest' of the UK political economy, increased as the City of London (which was increasingly integrated with Wall Street in the USA) came to benefit from the liberalisation of global capital markets and the persistence of a light-touch regulatory regime. This growth typified the growth of the services sector more generally, as the manufacturing sector declined throughout the post-war period, but the vast majority of service sector jobs were located in low value-added industries. The public sector became extremely important to the UK growth model during the 2000s, especially in Wales and the

North of England, by way of mitigating de-development in these areas and stimulating consumer demand through the creation of public sector jobs. Household consumption was a significantly more important dimension of the UK economy than most comparable countries, but, given the relative lack of high-paying industries, was dependent upon household indebtedness, either directly through consumer borrowing or indirectly through the withdrawal of equity from a booming housing market (boosted by low interest rates, mortgage market liberalisation, and a chronic housing undersupply).

The persistence of the UK's non-interventionist industrial policy, openness to foreign corporations, and financialised forms of corporate governance, a reversal of employment protection laws, and relatively high immigration contributed to many of the hallmarks of the growth model during this period, such as a significant trade deficit, the vulnerability of many regions and industries to exogenous shocks, and limited earnings growth for low- and middle-income households. A conservative approach to fiscal policy, which forms the *raison d'être* of HM Treasury, the most powerful part of the state apparatus, was also strongly reasserted during this period. High levels of public services investment were only made possible by increasing tax receipts from the finance sector, and an enhanced role for private finance in the public sector (Berry 2013). The growth model was underpinned ideologically by the assumptions and prescriptions of 'neoliberalism'. Colin Hay (2013) describes the model as 'Anglo-liberal' to signal both the long standing influence of a classical liberal ideology, and the affinity (and integration) between the UK economy and those elsewhere in the English-speaking world. However, it is crucial to note that few of its principal stewards were self-conscious adherents to such ideological categories. When considering the role of ideational phenomena in supporting and constituting the growth model, it is more accurate to speak of a small number of core concepts that have long framed UK economic statecraft, such as a quintessential commitment to individual property rights, influenced by both a liberal valorisation of individualism and a conservative valorisation of an unequal social order. Both of these traditions also help explain the UK polity's support for the idea of a competitive marketplace as the organising principle of capitalism, which was largely uncontested during the decades immediately prior to the financial crisis. The specific commitment to property rights above all other entitlement-based claims was an often unspoken influence on policies that impacted upon housing, or which incentivised home ownership.

The UK's long standing openness to international trade and investment activity intensified during this period, manifest as a profound commitment to and positive representation of the apparent process of 'globalisation'. The effective institutionalisation of many of these ideational commitments served to moderate left-wing political programmes, yet it would be wrong not to recognise the integral role of some social democratic ideas on the growth model, particularly as adapted under New Labour, notably the importance of welfarism in justifying the state's subsidisation of stagnant private sector earnings through tax credits.

The growth model was severely challenged by the financial crisis which peaked in autumn 2008, followed by a severe recession and sporadic recovery. Consistent GDP growth only returned in late 2013. However, even this upturn was associated with rapid population growth (chiefly due to immigration); GDP per capita did not recover to its pre-crisis peak until the middle of 2015. The financial crisis was triggered by debt defaults in the sub-prime mortgage market in the USA. The UK bank Northern Rock had been heavily exposed to this market, and its collapse, alongside several American lenders, in fact helped to intensify the crisis on Wall Street, which led to a significant decline in value for all mortgage-backed securities, and eventually caused the effective insolvency of the entire Anglo-American banking sector as interbank lending ceased. It is impossible to know how significantly the crisis would have affected the major UK banks were they not so heavily exposed to American capital markets—yet this issue is clearly moot, given that Anglo-American financial integration was integral to the role of the London-based finance sector within the UK growth model. Furthermore, we can be certain that underlying demand weaknesses in the UK economy started to materialise from the mid-2000s onwards, as wage stagnation placed an unsustainable weight on debt-based household consumption to fuel growth—an arrangement further strained by the need to raise interest rates to curb inflationary pressures associated with rising oil prices.

The Labour government's decision to recapitalise the UK banking sector in late 2008 was a direct response to the grave and immediate threat to the sector. But it was also a key moment in a larger story about how integral the availability of cheap credit had become to the UK growth model, and how fragile the balance sheets of the banks enabling this scenario were. The policy of quantitative easing (QE), through which the Bank of England purchases UK government bonds with new electronic money, served the dual purpose of keeping the cost of government borrowing low, but also to artificially boost the value of other assets, such as company shares, to stimulate business confidence. Clearly, QE is an extraordinary policy which contravenes the conservative form of economic statecraft that had become conventional in the pre-crisis period. The banking bailout, followed by QE, meant that the UK finance sector was preserved largely intact, and the capital markets upon which it depends were shielded from the worst effects of the downturn. Yet it was immediately clear that the sector would struggle to serve as the motor for economic growth in the short to medium term.

The identification of economic growth as the ostensible objective of the economic and political institutions of which the growth model consists marks out the concept as more than simply a conflation of the Marxist regulation school and the varieties of capitalism approach. It follows that the key finding of analysis to date of the apparent failure of the UK growth model in 2008 was that it was a crisis *of growth*. The finding necessarily and deliberately contradicted the view expounded by policymaking elites, particularly the ascendant Conservative Party, that the crisis was *of debt*, and specifically public debt. It is perhaps reasonable to suppose that, if UK economic statecraft was attuned to the delivery of growth above all else, the clear failure of the economy to grow, as its main sources of growth were impeded, should have been elites' primary concern—and it is reasonable therefore to speculate whether the assumptions underpinning analysis of the growth model are unsound. Yet this paradox actually demonstrates rather well the analytical force of the growth model concept. Recognising a growth crisis would have required that an alternative growth model be forged. The closest elites got to this kind of agenda was the recognition that the UK economy required 'rebalancing', although this critique proved to be a fairly tame one (Berry and Hay 2014).

Clearly, if growth models were so easily disposable, they would be unworthy of the term. Growth models house patterns of accumulation, and forms of wealth distribution, that shape the political forces that ultimately determine which individuals and groups serve as the growth model's principal stewards. It is in this way that growth models become 'institutionalised'. To recognise that there exists a crisis of growth, even while growth is blatantly faltering according to the model-consistent formulae devised to monitor it, would be anathema to the elites that owe their status to the successful functioning of the model. It is vital that the notion that growth models are oriented towards delivering economic growth is divorced analytically from the notion that economic growth is synonymous with prosperity and progress. To reiterate, growth models are configured not to create wealth in a sustainable manner—although they may achieve this—but rather to maintain the statistical illusion of wealth creation, so that a given distribution of wealth can be maintained. The absence of statistical growth is therefore not as fatal to growth models as we might logically assume, in part because such scenarios do not necessarily undermine the wealth of the groups that sustain the growth model, and in part because this failure can be effectively obscured through the influence of elites over the production and dissemination of knowledge about the economy.

This is not to suggest that agents and alternative ideas are incapable of challenging the structures represented by the growth model—but to think that they may do so, or may *only* do so, at times of apparent crisis would be to misunderstand the complex interaction of structure and agency, and material and ideational, and indeed overlook the possibility that a declaration of crisis may serve the interests of defending the existing growth model (Hay 1996, 2002). As such, the task that fell to policymaking elites in 2008 became one of shoring up the existing growth model. As this book demonstrates, model continuity came at the price of significant modifications in prevailing forms of economic statecraft, particularly in the immediate wake of the financial crisis, but also from 2010 onwards. Yet the definition of the crisis as one of public debt—which happened quickly but not instantaneously—ensured this agenda could be pursued with relatively limited scrutiny, and less uncertainly than might otherwise have been the case. It is for this reason that austerity, rather than its conceptual relative rebalancing, is the organising concept of the UK's post-crisis political economy. Austerity is the post-crisis prescription, but also acts to define the problems that caused the crisis in the first place. Despite its deliberately uneconomic connotations, austerity has far more to do with the politics of economic growth than rebalancing does.

The Rediscovery of Austerity

All growth models encompass contradictions or, more precisely, dimensions that seem incongruous from the vantage of some of the coalition of ideological perspectives that buttress the model. The most obvious contradiction encompassed by the UK growth model in the pre-crisis period in this regard is the high level of public spending—especially given the cross-party consensus on maintaining relatively low rates of taxation on earnings, profits, and assets. While those on the right of the ideological spectrum never seriously challenged the extent of public expenditure in the decades immediately before the crisis, it seems obvious in hindsight that if the growth model were to be salvaged after 2008, a sacrificial lamb would be required. Labour's record on the public finances—or the simplistic interpretation of this record which eventually became part of the fabric of UK political discourse—was it, not least because it could be crudely associated with an overextension of the welfare state.

The blueprint for this narrative is of course not new, but rather one which has reoccurred at several points in the recent history of the UK, most notably during the interwar years. Mark Blyth (2013) in fact locates the origins of the economic doctrine of austerity in John Locke's late seventeenth-century liberalism—a veneration of individual property rights—and shows that it was widely adhered to not just in the UK but throughout Western Europe and North America in the early twentieth century. But it was not until late 2008, after the banks had been recapitalised, that then shadow chancellor George Osborne began to link discursively Labour's economic stewardship with high public spending—having complained very little about Gordon Brown's approach to fiscal policy before the financial crisis—and he did so, in an article in *The Financial Times*, in a characteristically disingenuous manner. He described Brown as presiding over an 'age of irresponsibility', and bemoaned that the UK had run in 2007/2008 'the highest budget deficit of any leading western country'. 'It is little wonder', he continued, 'that last week the International Monetary Fund joined the European Commission in predicting that Britain would suffer a deeper recession than any of our competitors' (Osborne 2008). Public spending was of course not the reason that the UK's recession was predicted to be deeper than most similar countries (a forecast born out in practice); rather, the reason was the UK economy's dependence on private debt and the housing market, coupled with the specific impact of the financial crisis on the availability of credit, as discussed above. Indeed, Osborne's article promises also to address 'growing levels of personal debt' and 'the overvalued UK housing market'. As will be shown in this book, neither objective went on to form a significant aspect of the Conservative Party's agenda in government, despite the rhetorical commitment to rebalancing. It was around this time that Osborne established the Office for Budget Responsibility (OBR)—later transposed into the Whitehall machinery—ostensibly to narrow his own room for fiscal manoeuvre as

Chancellor. The fact that the UK had in 2007 the lowest level of public debt among G7 countries, with the exception of Canada, is an inconvenient truth marginalised within the early austerity narrative. This is not to say that this claim, broadcast frequently by Gordon Brown in 2008 (and repeated ever since by the advocates of a Keynesian response to the downturn), is not misleading to some extent, because the Blair and Brown governments had become increasingly imprudent, in their own terms, as some elements of the growth model had begun to malfunction in the years preceding the crisis—which explains the growing budget deficit that Osborne referred to (see Chote et al. 2010). But it is not credible to associate this rather unremarkable trend with the severity of the subsequent recession.

The UK was not alone in pursuing some version of an austerity programme. The idea gained significant international support, particularly since the onset of the so-called Eurozone sovereign debt crisis in late 2009. Although the G20, under the influence of Gordon Brown, had initially taken a fairly relaxed approach to public spending—focusing instead on financial regulation—by 2010, the group was calling for '"growth friendly" fiscal consolidation' on a global scale (G20 2010). Of course, by 2009, the Brown government had also begun to make significant spending cuts domestically, undermining the impression that has arisen more recently of Brown as a late convert to Keynesianism, although overall public expenditure was rising due largely to increased social security spending. The International Monetary Fund (IMF) became one of the main advocates of significant public spending reductions around this time, not least because it was being called upon to provide emergency loans to many Eurozone countries, although the bulk of the funds were in fact provided, in a piecemeal and seemingly begrudging manner, by Eurozone members and the European Central Bank (ECB) through various mechanisms. The exposure of German banks to the public debt of most Eurozone members helps to explain the politics here: Germany wanted its banks to get their money back, but also to ensure that the debt-based assets on their balance sheets retained as much value as possible in the short term (Thompson 2013).

While the UK was initially seen as too 'hawkish' on spending cuts by the IMF, it was praised in 2010 for its 'forceful multi-year fiscal deficit reduction programme' which was forecast, somewhat comically, to enable 'a balanced and sustainable recovery… and is essential to ensure debt sustainability, thereby greatly reducing the risk of a costly loss of confidence in public finances. Fiscal tightening will dampen but not stop growth, as other sectors of the economy emerge as drivers of recovery' (IMF 2010). The IMF has subsequently censured itself over its turn to austerity in 2010; however, while it went on to strongly criticise, again, the UK government's hawkishness, it has also been surprised by the UK's positive growth statistics since 2013 (Independent Evaluation Office of the IMF 2014; Inman 2014). In the USA, Barack Obama has presided over a period of significant spending reductions, albeit implemented mostly at the local and state levels. A hostile Congress—typified by the repeated wrangles over the 'fiscal cliff' in the federal budget—has also restrained his own spending plans (Krugman 2014; Thompson 2012). In 2015, however, as his presidency neared its end, he proposed a new public investment programme and criticised the 'mindless austerity' of the past decade (Obama 2015). In the USA, and to some extent Australia, the UK has been consistently held up by progressive political actors as an example of austerity gone wrong, even if 'the basic picture remains one of shared rather than separate experience' (Clark 2015, p. 9). It is worth noting that in many of the Southern European countries perceived to have had austerity imposed on them externally by 'the Troika' of the IMF, European Commission, and ECB, populist movements advocating varying degrees of economic nationalism have emerged. The UK has seen no such trend on any significant scale (notwithstanding the election of Jeremy Corbyn as leader of the Labour Party)—at least in part because the UK's austerity politics is home-grown. There is little substantive international pressure on the UK to adopt a programme of austerity, unlike many members of the Eurozone or recipients of IMF loans; instead, austerity is an agenda which fits naturally with the outlook of UK policy elites.

But one of the key aims of this book is to consider whether austerity, as conventionally understood, has been applied systematically in the UK. In practice, Osborne's austerity agenda has offered both less *and* more than it initially appears. Firstly, central government's *ability* to control short-term expenditure and borrowing levels has probably been overstated. This is perhaps the main reason that Osborne was repeatedly forced to suspend the date at which the budget deficit and government borrowing would begin to fall—let alone be eliminated. In June 2010, Osborne had promised to eliminate the budget deficit and significantly reduce the national debt within the five years of the coalition government. The targets were revised forwards several times, with Osborne promising in his emergency budget of July 2015 to create a balanced budget by 2017/2018—but he forecast that the national debt would remain above 70 per cent of gross domestic product (GDP) by the end of the Conservative's first term as a majority government in 2020, that is, higher than the level he originally expected to have attained *by 2015* (OBR 2010, 2015b). That the coalition government consistently failed to meet its deficit reduction targets is unremarkable; yet their determination, despite this failure, to maintain the illusion of austerity is highly revealing. We can also question, secondly, the government's *willingness* to pursue austerity as conventionally understood. The coalition government pursued a highly selective cuts agenda which, while severe in some areas, has also seen spending increase in others, and taxation reduced for some individuals and private enterprises. This selectivity is due in part to its recognition of the economically destructive nature of any straightforward implementation of the publicly espoused austerity agenda (the recovery only resumed, in 2012, once Osborne's Plan A had been substantially relaxed), but also of the importance of the state's role—as detailed throughout this book—in protecting and promoting certain forms of economic activity.

Chapter Outline and Main Arguments

The book's contents arise from a two-year research project on the transformation of the UK growth model as a result of the financial crisis, considering primarily how dominant economic forms have been challenged or indeed reinforced by economic policy. The next four chapters broadly represent the four key strands of this research, and the final main chapter represents the secondary objective of the research, that is, considering what forms of political action and public policy could enable progressive change. The research has been primarily inductive in nature, seeking to discern patterns of political and economic change from the examination of various sources, rather than seeking answers to specific questions designated a priori. The sources examined fall broadly into two camps: firstly, policy-related documents, including public statements by politicians, accessed for information on both the nature of policy change and how it was being justified, and secondly, evidence of the impact of financial crisis and subsequent policy change on economic activity, drawing primarily upon official statistics, but supplemented by non-governmental sources of evidence where necessary.

The focus of the book is primarily on the Conservative Party in government since 2010, first in coalition with the Liberal Democrats, and then forming a majority government after the 2015 general election. It also emphasises one particularly salient aspect of the research described above, that is, the ideological dimension of recent economic policy practice. As such, the focus is in large part upon what the Conservative Party has sought to achieve in policy terms via the invocation of the idea of austerity. The core argument regarding how post-crisis economic policy can be characterised is relatively simple: the Conservative Party has pursued 'radical continuity', that is, significant policy change, in order to defend an existing growth model. Detailing what this looks like in practice is less straightforward, not least because policymakers rarely have complete autonomy to implement their agenda exactly as they would wish. This is where the ideological realm becomes paramount, as hegemony over ideas enables political actors to create the space for their policy objectives. As such, the role played by the austerity narrative has been crucial to the goal of re-legitimating the key aspects of the UK's pre-crisis growth model. Firstly, it indicates the incapacity of the state to intervene in the economy in a way which contravenes perceived market forces, by implying that the state itself has no capacity to create wealth. Secondly, it reinforces the need for certain behaviours at the individual level which conform to the short-termist, profit-seeking (and rent-seeking) activities of the private sector, by implying that individual indiscipline is the chief cause of socio-economic disadvantage. Crucially, the ideological connotations of austerity have also been instrumental in narrowing the space for the articulation of a centre-left alternative to the Conservative Party's policy programme.

The book proceeds in five main parts. The second chapter focuses on monetary policy and the wider policy agenda around financial services. It argues that the UK growth model encompasses a process of 'financialisation'. The austerity agenda is in large part designed to protect and advance this process, despite the centrality of finance to the 2008 crisis, by restricting the fiscal role of the state and compelling individuals to engage with the housing market and financial services. Yet these objectives require higher spending and/or greater fiscal risks, arguably contradicting the conventional understanding of austerity. The third chapter focuses on industrial policy and the closely related area of regional policy, both of which heavily feature in the coalition and Conservative governments' agenda around 'rebalancing' the UK economy. It argues, however, that rebalancing, despite first impressions, does not endorse a critique of either finance-led growth or *laissez-faire* industrial and regional policy. Instead, it valorises the market economy and acts to further delegitimise the notion of the state (both locally and nationally) as a purposeful economic actor and, as such, complements the master narrative around austerity. The fourth chapter looks at welfare reform and the employability agenda. It argues that while the retrenchment of welfare entitlements has been central to the austerity narrative, reducing expenditure on social security benefits has not. This helps to reveal, as the chapter further explores, the relationship between austerity, employment policy, and the exacerbation of problems related to pay and job insecurity in the UK economy.

The fifth chapter considers the coalition and Conservative governments' apparent objectives around eliminating the budget deficit and reducing borrowing. It argues that despite their clear success in the debates around macroeconomic theory, Keynesian economists have exaggerated the centrality of deficit reduction to the austerity agenda and, as such, offer us only a partial understanding of the latter's character as a fiscal policy agenda. In practice, deficit reduction, even if never achieved, functions as a legitimising mechanism for the wider objectives of austerity. The establishment of the OBR offers a case in point: ostensibly focused on assessing progress towards deficit reduction, the OBR actually serves to institutionalise austerity within the machinery of government by legitimising the assumptions built into the deficit reduction agenda. The sixth chapter considers what impact austerity has had across the political spectrum, by analysing how dominant economic policy discourses have been present in apparent attempts to oppose the Conservative Party's policy agenda. It argues that the significantly disparate nature of the varied perspectives on how (and why) austerity should be challenged, both within the Labour Party and beyond, is a demonstration of just how successful it has been as a governing philosophy in undermining social democratic alternatives to neoliberalism. The ideas and groups that seem to have had the most success in challenging the Conservatives' ideological hegemony have been those that have strongly articulated localist or nationalist sentiment. However, while such initiatives often adopt anti-austerity rhetoric, they do not in practice offer a direct challenge to its assumptions. Finally, the book concludes by summarising the main arguments, via further reflection on the relationship between austerity and economic crises, and what this tells us about the present and future of the UK growth model.

References

Berry, C. (2011). *Globalisation and ideology in Britain: Neoliberalism, free trade and the global economy*. Manchester: Manchester University Press.

Berry, C. (2013). Are we there yet? Growth, rebalancing and the pseudo-recovery. Sheffield Political Economy Research Institute paper no. 7. http://speri.dept.shef.ac.uk/wp-content/uploads/2013/01/SPERI-Paper-No.7-Are-We-There-Yet-PDF-747KB.pdf. Accessed 31 Jul 2015.

Berry, C., & Hay, C. (2014). The great British 'rebalancing' act: The construction and implementation of an economic imperative for exceptional times. *British Journal of Politics and International Relations*, published online 12 December 2014. http://dx.doi.org/10.1111/1467-856X.12063

Blyth, M. (2013). *Austerity: The history of a dangerous idea*. Oxford: Oxford University Press.

Chote, R., Crawford, R., Emmerson, C., & Tetlow, G. (2010). *The public finances: 1997 to 2010*. Institute for Fiscal Studies Election Briefing Note no. 6. http://www.ifs.org.uk/bns/bn93.pdf. Accessed 31 Jul 2015.

Clark, T. (2015). *Hard times: Inequality, recession and aftermath*. London: Yale University Press.

G20 (G20). (2010). *The G20 Toronto Summit declaration*. http://www.g20.utoronto.ca/2010/to-communique.html. Accessed 31 Jul 2015.

Hall, P., & Soskice, D. (2001). *Varieties of capitalism: The institutional foundations of comparative advantage*. Oxford: Oxford University Press.

Hay, C. (1996). Narrating crisis: The discursive construction of the winter of discontent. *Sociology, 30*(2), 253–277.

Hay, C. (2002). *Political analysis*. Basingstoke: Palgrave MacMillan.

Hay, C. (2013). *The failure of Anglo-liberal capitalism*. Basingstoke: Palgrave.

Independent Evaluation Office of the International Monetary Fund. (2014). *IMF response to the financial and economic crisis*. http://www.ieo-imf.org/ieo/files/completedevaluations/FULL%20REPORT%20final.pdf. Accessed 31 Jul 2015.

Inman, P. (2014). IMF predicts Britain's GDP growth rate will surge to 3.2% by year end. *The Guardian*, July 24. http://www.theguardian.com/business/2014/jul/24/imf-predicts-britain-gdp-growth-rate-surge. Accessed 31 Jul 2015.

International Monetary Fund. (2010). *United Kingdom: 2010*. International Monetary Fund country report no. 10/338. https://www.imf.org/external/pubs/ft/scr/2010/cr10338.pdf. Accessed 31 Jul 2015.

Jessop, B. (1990). *State theory: Putting the capitalist state in its place*. Cambridge: Polity.

Krugman, P. (2014). The Obama recovery. *The New York Times*, December 28. http://www.nytimes.com/2014/12/29/opinion/paul-krugman-the-obama-recovery.html. Accessed 31 Jul 2015.

Obama, B. (2015). Remarks by the President on the FY2016 budget. Speech delivered on 2 February 2015. https://www.whitehouse.gov/the-press-office/2015/02/02/remarks-president-fy2016-budget. Accessed 31 Jul 2015.

Office for Budget Responsibility. (2010). *Budget forecast: June 2010*. http://budgetresponsibility.org.uk/budget-2010/. Accessed 31 Jul 2015.

Office for Budget Responsibility. (2015b). *Economic and fiscal outlook: July 2015*. http://budgetresponsibility.org.uk/economic-fiscal-outlook-july-2015/. Accessed 31 Jul 2015.

Osborne, G. (2008). How Britain should tackle its recession. *Financial Times*, 9 November. https://next.ft.com/content/0171d590-ae8f-11dd-b621-000077b07658. Accessed 11 Apr 2016.

Thompson, D. (2012). Barack Obama, austerity president. *The Atlantic*, 1 February 2015. http://www.theatlantic.com/business/archive/2012/02/barack-obama-austerity-president/252319/. Accessed 31 Jul 2015.

Thompson, H. (2013). The crisis of the Euro: The problem of German power revisited. Sheffield Political Economy Research Institute paper no. 8. http://speri.dept.shef.ac.uk/wp-content/uploads/2013/01/SPERI-Paper-NO.8-The-Crisis-of-the-Euro-The-Problem-of-German-Power-Revisited-PDF-536KB.pdf. Accessed 31 Jul 2015.

CHAPTER 2

Financialisation and the Property-Owning Autocracy

Abstract UK policy-makers' interventionist response to the financial crisis might suggest that the hold of neoliberal ideology over elites' understanding of and prescriptions for the economy had loosened. However, we need to understand the defining role of the process of 'financialisation', and the integral function of the housing market, within the pre-crisis growth model. Interventions by policy elites have predominantly served to support financialisation and the housing market. The austerity agenda pursued most forcefully since 2010 is designed to protect and advance financialisation, by further undermining the legitimacy of fiscal policy interventions—even though the resurrection of the pre-crisis growth model has required significant and novel fiscal manoeuvres by central government. Austerity has also justified an intensification of the compulsion for individuals to engage with finance.

Keywords Financialisation • Housing market • Austerity • Monetary activism • Fiscal risks • Debt

UK policymakers' highly interventionist response to the financial crisis—initiated by the Labour government in 2008 but largely upheld by the coalition and Conservative majority governments since 2010—might, in some senses, suggest that the hold of neoliberal ideology over elites'

C. Berry, *Austerity Politics and UK Economic Policy*, Building a Sustainable Political Economy: SPERI Research & Policy,
DOI 10.1057/978-1-137-59010-7_2

understanding of and prescriptions for the economy had loosened. Of course, even during the height of neoliberalism's influence in the 1980s, 1990s, and early 2000s, the state had been an interventionist and enabling state; capitalist economies, even market-based varieties, cannot function any other way. Yet the assumption that there were fairly strict limits to the state's economic functions, and indeed something *un*economic about the state itself, was pervasive. The panic induced by the collapse of Lehman Brothers in September 2008 did not mean that policy conventions decades in the making were suddenly discarded, and the imprint of neoliberalism on the policy responses to the crisis is unmistakable. The baby was most certainly not thrown out with the bathwater. Nevertheless, state intervention was absolutely and conspicuously paramount to 'rescuing' the UK economy—as elsewhere, to a lesser extent—from some degree of irreparable damage.

This does not necessarily mean the end of neoliberalism, but rather one type of neoliberalism. In his book *Never Let a Serious Crisis Go to Waste*, Philip Mirowski (2014) distinguishes between 'Austrian' and 'monetarist' neoliberalism, arguing that a seemingly purer form of neoliberalism, embodied in the so-called Austrian school of economics and close in sentiment to libertarianism, would have allowed the crisis to run a 'natural' course, with limited state intervention. Failing banks, and perhaps entire financial districts, would have collapsed, but, so the logic goes, something better would have risen from the ashes. In contrast, the monetarist neoliberals were never particularly enamoured with the competitive efficiencies of unregulated markets, but rather committed to supporting private enterprise, and its profitability, by whatever means necessary. Invariably, this meant creating cheap credit, and socialising risks that the Austrian school theoretically believed should have been borne by the market itself. The response to the crisis in the UK was therefore very much to type for monetarist neoliberals and, as such, in Mirowski's terms, neoliberalism 'survived'. What Mirowski is outlining of course is not two alternative branches of neoliberal thought, but rather the difference between neoliberalism as a philosophy and neoliberalism as a 'real world' phenomenon, advocated and implemented by actual political actors. This is not to suggest that the latter is a diluted version of the former. For political economists, it is arguably just as plausible to think of the line of causation running in the other direction, or both directions at the same time; the beneficiaries of neoliberalism in practice were well-served by the invocation of the market and competition as the organising motifs of economic life, even if they were actually applied unevenly, and so created the intellectual space for the purer version of neoliberalism to be disseminated.

This is not the place to adjudicate on whether 'monetarist neoliberalism' is a useful term for understanding the nature of crisis responses in political economies like the UK. The broader lesson is that the 2008 crisis elicited an enormous programme of state intervention in order to maintain in large part the growth model which defined the pre-crisis period. This chapter argues that the growth model encompassed and advanced a process of 'financialisation'. This process incorporates economic, political, and cultural dimensions and is defined here expansively as encompassing the enhanced role and status of the finance sector in the economy, an intensified focus of most private economic actors on short-term financial returns, greater interaction between individuals and financial services, and the personalisation of financial risks as collectivised risk-sharing mechanisms are dismantled (Berry 2015). As William Davies has argued, the state has always been central to the process of financialisation, not only in maintaining the role and status of the finance sector to an extent which a purely market-driven agenda would not have permitted, but also in creating new markets for financial services, as the influence of welfarism on the neoliberal state necessitated policies to bring about financial inclusion (Davies 2014; see also Berry 2015). In this sense, there are 'limits' to what is conventionally understood as neoliberalism. The purpose of this chapter is to show that the austerity agenda is firmly implanted in this intellectual and political landscape, by discussing how this dynamic manifests in actual economic policy practice. After briefly discussing the role of the housing market in the process of financialisation and the UK growth model, the chapter focuses on post-crisis monetary policy practice, before turning finally to the broader agenda around financial services.

Austerity and the Housing Market

The housing market is central to key aspects of the process of financialisation in the UK. Through home ownership, people are exposed to various housing market risks, chiefly the impact of house prices on their asset wealth, and usually the impact of interest rates on their disposable income—therefore ensuring that their short- and long-term well-being is bound up in housing. Of course, in a housing system organised around home ownership, with only a limited role for social housing among rental properties, the risks of not owning a home are arguably greater. The purchase of property through mortgage debt creates an intimate link between individuals and financial services, with the banking sector serving as both facilitator of access to the housing market and enforcer of its constraining logic. Crucially, the proliferation of mortgage debt in the late 1990s and early 2000s, aided by public policies often justified as egalitarian in nature, became vital to the operation of Anglosphere finance sectors, in enabling new forms of securitisation. This indicates the centrality of the housing market to the pre-crisis growth model. In fact, housing played a much more direct role in the growth model through the financing of consumption, especially as earnings growth stagnated. During 2006, as the pre-crisis housing market peaked, more than £37 billion was 'withdrawn' by UK households from housing equity, equivalent to around 5 per cent of household consumption. It had hovered close to this level (in terms of proportion of consumption) in the late 1980s, but housing equity withdrawal was generally negligible or negative (meaning equity was being created) throughout the 1990s, before rising sharply from 2001 onwards.[1]

It is debatable whether the housing market is now playing the same role: housing equity withdrawal has been strongly negative since late 2008. However, analysis by the Bank of England has suggested that this is due not to a fundamental transformation of the wider economic role of housing wealth, but rather the fact that fewer housing transactions are taking place (undermining opportunities for withdrawal), and the impact of 'Help to Buy' (HTB) in its initial form on the construction of new homes (Berry and Hay 2014, p. 17). To pre-empt the discussion below, it seems fair to conclude that the coalition and Conservative governments have attempted to restore the role of the housing market in this regard, especially as earnings growth has continued to stagnate, even if they have not yet succeeded. Crucially, housing equity need not actually be withdrawn to fuel consumption: as house prices rise—as they continue to—homeowners are made to *feel* richer, in the sense that they have greater confidence that they are safely accumulating wealth. Furthermore, although it is impossible to verify this from the available data, housing equity withdrawal may be strongly supporting the consumption of some groups, even if the figures suggest that this is not happening at the aggregate level. We know, for instance, that the recovery in average house prices since the financial crisis has been heavily skewed towards London and the South East (Berry and Hay 2014, pp. 16, 17). This actually tells us something even more significant about the role of the housing market in the UK growth model.

It is not simply the case that housing wealth supports a particular growth strategy, but also that it enables the maintenance of an unequal distribution of wealth. Countless studies have in recent years detailed extensive (and growing) inequality in housing wealth evident in the UK; the Office for National Statistics' (ONS) Wealth and Assets Survey (WAS) is the most authoritative source, albeit limited in terms of assessing the wealth of the very, very wealthy. Nevertheless, the 2010/2012 WAS shows that the top decile of households in terms of total wealth held more than £1.3 trillion in net property wealth, almost as much as the bottom eight deciles combined (ONS 2014b). Of course, the values that underpin the UK growth model are remarkably successful in legitimising this inequality through the production of 'common sense'. While many would agree that this distribution is regrettable, it is nevertheless accepted as a by-product of individuals and families simply seeking to secure for themselves a nice place to live and the semblance of financial security, unblemished by culpability for the structure of the housing market at the macro level.

Home ownership is clearly a disciplining condition for most people—both those who own property through mortgage lending, and indeed those seeking to 'get a foot on the housing ladder'. The long standing conservative ideal of a 'property-owning democracy', re-popularised by Margaret Thatcher in the 1970s and 1980s, implies that a society in which most people own their own home would be more equitable, yet it is equally clear that such an arrangement would also be valuable insofar as people who are more intimately invested in the fortunes of the national economy are less likely to want to put their stake at risk through radical politics. The property-owning democracy is therefore rather undemocratic, in that it disciplines individuals against both alternative approaches to economic policy as well as the option of not participating in the labour market and is perhaps better characterised as an 'autocracy' founded on the unquestioned logic of housing wealth accumulation. Austerity discourse undoubtedly reinforces this logic. Even while the state appears to be playing as significant a role as ever in supporting the housing market, including facilitating access to mortgage lending, the idea of austerity reminds us, firstly, that the state cannot be relied upon as a housing provider (even one of last resort) and, secondly, that the primary responsibility for acquiring the security of home ownership resides at the individual level. Austerity therefore clearly reinforces the multidimensional process of financialisation. Individuals are encouraged to consider their personal financial well-being above all other considerations and enter into intimate financial relationships with the banking sector in the process. The state moves further towards the monetarist neoliberal model outlined by Mirowski by paradoxically protecting the housing market against the competitive pressures of supply and demand and, at the same time, replenishing mortgage lenders' customer base through the apparent democratisation of financial inclusion. Yet it does so *under the cloak of not doing so*, as austerity ensures that the notion that the state may do anything other than help us to help ourselves is comprehensively demonised.

The Meaning of Monetary Activism

The main, direct policy connotations of the discourse around austerity relate to fiscal policy. As explored at greatest length in Chap. 5, the idea explicitly prescribes lower public spending, although its primary objective probably relates to reducing public borrowing. At the same time, the most significant economic policy changes enacted by the coalition and Conservative governments appear to relate to monetary policy. David Cameron (2013) repeated in a speech his self-diagnosis as a fiscal conservative but monetary activist—the juxtaposition was also employed by George Osborne in his party conference speech (Osborne 2011). The argument here is that the monetary activism in evidence under the coalition and Conservative governments is rather exceptional in nature. Parts of it include the state shouldering greater *fiscal* risks. This is, to some extent, Keynesian history repeating itself: John Maynard Keynes (1919) argued that at times of crisis, monetary policy becomes largely indistinguishable from fiscal policy in its role in macroeconomic management. As such, while the Conservative strategy is not historically unprecedented in this regard, what is more novel is that they have sought to entirely discredit the notion of the state's fiscal role being employed in boosting economic recovery, even as monetary policy is effectively 'fiscalised'.

Quantitative easing (QE) is the most obvious example of monetary activism under the coalition, and a rather straightforward (but underreported) case of the boundaries between monetary and fiscal policy becoming blurred. QE was of course first introduced in 2009 as part of the Labour government's immediate response to the financial crisis, following the banking 'bailout' in 2008. Yet almost half of the Bank of England's (hereafter 'the Bank') £375 billion of asset purchases associated with QE has come after 2010, when the early signs of economic recovery evaporated in 2011. The final round came in summer 2012.

QE involves the creation of new money electronically for the purposes of purchasing UK government gilts from the private sector—that is, the state effectively nationalising its own debt. The explicit aim of QE is to encourage the initial 'recipients' to purchase other assets in place of the nationalised gilts, primarily equities in listed companies, in order to enable greater investment by the ultimate beneficiaries and higher consumption by equity owners. Insofar as QE increases demand for UK gilts (to replace those purchased by the Bank), the programme also has the additional implication of reducing the cost of government borrowing. Arguably, this has been its main achievement, with evidence of its success in stimulating demand in the real economy far more mixed. We should not be surprised by this, given QE's dependence on 'trickle down' economics. The effect anticipated by the Bank of England was that higher asset prices would stimulate spending by increasing the wealth of asset holders, that is, those with significant capital market holdings (Green and Lavery 2015, pp. 11, 12; Joyce et al. 2011). We can speculate that although the Bank appears somewhat mournful about QE's boost to the wealthiest groups (Bank of England 2012), the role of QE in sustaining patterns of wealth distribution, facilitated by engagement with UK capital markets, that had been threatened by the financial crisis, is more than simply incidental.

The use of QE is of course not unique to the UK—it was used, for instance, in Japan in the 1990s, in the USA from 2008 onwards, and very recently, by the European Central Bank. However, there appear to be few other contexts where the ascetic imagery of austerity contrasts so sharply with profligacy in practice. The fiscal risk associated with QE is rarely acknowledged by policymakers and has attracted little critical attention. Essentially, insofar as central banks are uncomfortable owning enormous volumes of government debt, the withdrawal of QE would require gilts being sold back to the private sector. But if interest rates have risen materially by that point (which is the intention of the Bank), the assets in question will be significantly less valuable than the point at which they were purchased. From a fiscal perspective, QE therefore encompasses a radical deficit spending programme. Of course, the fiscal deficit associated with QE will never really materialise, because, as the Bank confirmed in 2014, QE will not be withdrawn when interest rates are high. The £375 billion stock will be 'maintained' until the bank rate has once again risen, so that it could then be cut to enable risk-free withdrawal (Bank of England 2014). The logic of this position is such that QE could theoretically be withdrawn presently, while the bank rate remains at rock bottom, but this seems incredibly unlikely; as discussed below, policy elites are now prioritising raising interest rates, before they think about reducing them once again at some undefined point. There is another almost entirely overlooked fiscal dimension of QE: the interest that the Treasury, as debtor, nominally pays to its creditor, the Bank of England, has since 2012 actually been paid instead to the Treasury (in other words, itself). This is in line with practice in Japan and the USA, but again demonstrates the strangeness of the relationship between monetary activism and austerity. Monetary activism is necessary because austerity prohibits fiscal activism. Yet since a large chunk of its debt interest payments are to itself, monetary activism in the form of QE actually makes austerity in the form of deficit reduction less necessary.

Paradoxically, both the severe fiscal risk *and* the abnormal fiscal benefits mean that QE may well never be withdrawn, at least not in any meaningful way. Certainly, it is hard to imagine the bank rate returning to a point as low as the present moment, having risen substantially in the intervening period. Perhaps more precisely, it is hard to imagine such a scenario which is not precipitated by another economic downturn, during which the possibility of withdrawing QE related to the previous crisis is unlikely to be deemed wise. The radical reduction in interest rates in 2008 was hugely important to salvaging key elements of the pre-crisis growth model. Low rates have supported lending by the banking sector, particularly mortgage lending, and crucially, helped UK banks to recapitalise relatively inexpensively in the face of asset write-downs, regulatory fines and compensation claims, and the strengthening of capital adequacy rules. The coalition government was keen to demonstrate its commitment to maintaining interest rates at historically low levels for the foreseeable future, by appointing Mark Carney as Governor of the Bank of England in 2013. Carney had been responsible for the policy of 'forward guidance' when in the equivalent role in his native Canada; forward guidance communicates the central bank's intention to maintain low interest rates until certain milestones in the economic recovery are met. Somewhat comically, Carney's main milestone, unemployment falling below 7 per cent, was met two years earlier than anticipated (demonstrating the inability of neoclassical economic models to explain labour market restructuring in the UK), while other measures such as productivity and earnings remained below expectation. As such, forward guidance was quietly discarded in a formal sense, so that, paradoxically, the policy of very low interest rates could continue.

The situation has evolved, not least because monetary activism has unleashed dynamics that, although entirely predictable, UK policy elites seem unable to manage. The Bank and George Osborne have both expressed a desire to see interest rates 'normalise' in the not-too-distant future, a formulation which is code for fears about the housing market radically outpacing the rest of the economy. This does not signal the abandonment of the pre-crisis growth model, but rather an attempt to breed confidence that the model has now been secured. Of course, low earners—who remain more abundant than elites expected—would struggle to cope with even a small increase in the cost of servicing their debts, and as such (in yet another paradox of austerity) the need for caution has been voiced most loudly on the left (cf. Kelly 2013; Dolphin 2014). The need for caution has also found support within the Bank of England in the form of its Chief Economist Andy Haldane, who was publicly rebuked by Carney for expressing concern about an 'early' rate rise (Reuters 2015). The Bank's dominant position is as revealing as it is strange. Arguing that rate rises can take up to two years to take effect, it argues that unless rates rise soon, it could be too late to act in time to confront rising inflation once it becomes evident (cf. Forbes 2015). Controlling inflation is of course the Bank's Monetary Policy Committee's (MPC) primary obligation, yet it seems odd to be worrying about reducing inflation at a time when inflation remains significantly below the MPC's 2 per cent target, and the spectre of deflation haunts many Western economies (Gamble 2014). Although very low inflation makes higher levels of investment—a prerequisite of higher productivity—far less likely, we can conclude that UK policy elites are generally more concerned about the hypothetical threat of high inflation to asset values. Maintaining low inflation also has the benefit of obscuring wage stagnation.

The coalition government's Funding for Lending Scheme (FLS) and HTB programme are also routinely associated with monetary activism, yet in practice also represent fiscal interventions. FLS was introduced in 2012 to counter the ongoing 'credit crunch' as UK banks continued to demonstrate a reluctance to lend. FLS was originally designed to facilitate higher volumes of lending to both businesses and homebuyers in the form of mortgages, but was restricted to business lending after the introduction of HTB. The scheme has been extended several times and is due to continue until at least 2016. Under the FLS, banks are able to swap their assets for short-term government debt via Treasury bills, via the Bank of England. The essentially risk-free nature of Treasury bills means banks can lend with a more secure capital. The 'assets' in question, however, are in fact the loans that are being made to firms (and previously individuals). Although the swapped loans have to be lower in value than the bills acquired, ostensibly protecting the fiscal balance sheet, the state is liable if the loans default. It is clear that policy elites are choosing to enable lending by loading risk onto the state, rather than, for instance, considering whether the structure of the UK banking sector constitutes a barrier to business lending.

HTB, launched in 2013, follows a similar pattern. It is presented as a technocratic adjustment, in the manner of monetary policy, but instead represents a sizeable programme of fiscal intervention. In the first phase of HTB (extended to 2020), applicable only to the purchase of new-build houses, the state offered heavily discounted loans of up to 20 per cent of property value to first-time buyers who had a deposit of at least 5 per cent of the value, with the remaining 75 per cent secured via a mortgage. The second, more controversial phase of HTB (due to end in 2016) sees the state guarantee entire mortgages, available from a limited range of suppliers, for homebuyers with a deposit of only 5 per cent. HTB is limited in England to properties purchased for £600,000 or less—yet this is more than triple the average house price in England and Wales when HTB was launched, exposing the underlying rationale of HTB, that is, to boost house prices, including in areas that had already experienced a strong housing market recovery, rather than merely to assist low-earners in purchasing a first home. HTB has succeeded in pushing up prices, therefore contributing to the problem it is ostensibly designed to solve (Allen and Pickard 2015). Ostensibly, the cost of HTB is negligible, assuming that loans are repaid, and may nominally improve the UK's fiscal position (lifetime scheme costs are classified as around £20 billion by the Treasury). Yet if the housing bubble the scheme arguably contributes to happens to burst (hardly an unlikely prospect), the state's liabilities will be significant. Together, FLS and HTB, as examples of fiscal policy (albeit masquerading as monetary policy), reinforce key elements of financialisation in the UK: the privileging of the banking sector, a recovery predicated on private debt, and the centrality of the housing market to growth.

Financialisation and Everyday Discipline

The coalition and Conservative governments have been active in ensuring that the disciplining role of financialisation upon individual behaviour has continued, and indeed intensified, since the financial crisis. Indeed, it can be argued that the largely macroeconomic agenda discussed in the previous section has been necessary to maintain the basic architecture through which financialisation at the individual level can be advanced, that is, intimate engagement with financial services and ultimately capital markets. In practice, of course, the macro and micro agendas align to buttress the UK's finance-centred growth model and unequal distribution of wealth. The concept of austerity has been more directly relevant to public discourse around the micro agenda than that around policies such as QE; however, this does not mean that this agenda conforms to austerity as it is conventionally understood.

Support for home ownership, discussed throughout this chapter, is the most obvious example in this regard. Home ownership is clearly a disciplining experience, insofar as relatively few homeowners actually own their homes, but instead mortgage them from the banking sector. HTB and related initiatives offer considerable fiscal support for individuals to become homeowners (taking on risks that the private sector was largely willing to shoulder before the crisis), but what is just as important, as noted above, is the denigration of the idea that the state might itself be thought of as a housing provider. The coalition and Conservative governments continue to incentivise local authorities to privatise their housing stock and, most controversially, have legislated to enforce the 'right to buy' to social housing tenants within the private sector, a policy which is likely to cause significant financial distress to private social housing providers. Of course, many people are unable to access the housing market and instead depend upon the private rental sector (also heavily subsidised by the state through Housing Benefit, with a third of the total budget, or £10 billion, paid directly to private landlords each year [Pickard 2014], as well as through various tax incentives). The process of renting is hardly less disciplining upon the individuals concerned in terms of everyday behaviour, although it ordinarily requires less acquiescence to the finance sector. But the more important point is that both the support for home ownership and the private rental market enable the continuation of the pre-crisis growth model through boosting house prices and circumventing the need for significant change within the UK banking sector's business models.

Home ownership is largely predicated upon private debt, although rarely acknowledged as such. However, challenging the prevalence of personal debt in general within the economy was an important dimension of the coalition government's early discourse around austerity, insofar as it chimed with the idea of individuals, as well as the state, living within their means. This line of argument crumbled fairly rapidly as the early signs of economic recovery dissipated in 2011, briefly creating an acute contradiction within

Conservative austerity discourse. For example, David Cameron's 2011 party conference speech claimed that UK households were paying off their credit card debts—yet official forecasters the Office for Budget Responsibility (OBR) was at the time predicting that household indebtedness would rise significantly in the next few years. Even more tellingly, and embarrassingly for Cameron, an earlier draft of the speech, released to the media in advance, revealed that he had intended to argue that people *should* be paying off their credit card debts. This was also contradicted by his own forecasters' analysis, as the OBR was at the time expecting consumption to rise faster than income, accounting for half of GDP growth by 2015, therefore requiring higher levels of debt (see OBR 2011a). Following Cameron's advice would have seen this path to recovery problematised. The economist Ann Pettifor (2013) has also documented the coalition government's wobbles on private debt, noting how the Treasury's complaint aired at the time of the 2011 budget that the UK economy was arguably the most indebted in the world, in terms of private debt, had disappeared a year later.

It is clear that policy elites are no longer particularly concerned about reducing private indebtedness: although the debt-to-income ratio for UK households fell to 136 per cent in 2014, from a pre-crisis high of 169, it is expected to move above 170 by 2020 (Berry and Hay 2015, p. 3). Beyond a strengthening of the regulatory regime around 'payday' lending in the face of significant media and parliamentary pressure, there have been few policy initiatives designed to curb indebtedness. We can speculate that this indifference is due to macroeconomic concerns around the possible impact of reducing indebtedness on consumption, even though it challenged the headline austerity motif. However, it is also worth considering whether private indebtedness came to play an important, but unacknowledged, role in the broader austerity agenda as it evolved under the coalition, insofar as it disciplines individuals, and cements a link between the notion of self-reliance and the actuality of reliance on financial services.

It has been slightly easier to justify the coalition and Conservative governments' support for pensions and general saving in terms of austerity—yet this does not mean that policy practice in these areas actually does conform unproblematically to austerity, as it might be conventionally understood. The coalition government continued with its predecessor's policy of 'automatic enrolment' into a private pension scheme, as fears about the implications of population ageing convinced the UK policy elite to seriously address the rapid decline in pensions saving since the 1980s. Yet the vast majority of auto-enrolees will join 'defined contribution' schemes, where investment risks are entirely individualised, rather than traditional, collectivist 'defined benefit' schemes where sponsoring employers themselves shoulder many of the associated risks. Moreover, many, if not most, will end up in oxymoronic 'group personal pensions', through which an employer chooses an insurance company to provide a pension product for its staff, but is then absolved of all responsibility for the resulting arrangements (beyond making contributions above a statutory minimum level). These products open up a new front in the mass roll-out of financialisation, as our retirement security becomes dependent upon intimate engagement with financial services, through products which are often indecipherable to ordinary savers. The coalition's liberalisation of the annuities market takes this agenda significantly further than New Labour had envisaged (defined contribution savers must purchase an annuity at retirement in order to convert their savings into a regular pension income). Defined contribution pensions clearly fit with notions of self-reliance and individuals taking greater responsibility for their own welfare—the fact that individuals have to opt out of schemes into which they are automatically enrolled by their employer, rather than being given an opportunity to opt in, indicates that individual choice is only a secondary dimension of the individualisation of pensions saving. Yet automatic enrolment can be seen to contradict austerity insofar as it necessitates a significant increase in public spending on pensions tax relief (Berry 2014a). The state, under the stewardship of the coalition and Conservative governments, is quite happy to spend more to realise the vision of economic life underpinning austerity discourse.

The Conservative agenda on supporting general saving has proceeded slightly differently; the coalition abandoned flagship New Labour policies in this area such as the Child Trust Fund (CTF) and the Saving Gateway (SG), which favoured or were exclusively focused on the poorest families. Yet it has sought to support saving for wealthier groups by making (from April 2016) the first £1,000 of interest earned on savings tax-free. However, this should not be understood as a pro-saving policy, in the sense that it might encourage saving rather than spending. The measure will make a negligible difference to poorer groups with a greater propensity to spend rather than save their income and who, in any case, are more likely to engage in consumer borrowing. Rather, it serves as partial compensation for wealthier groups (only those in the top 5 per cent of the income distribution will be ineligible for this support) for the continuation of downward pressure on interest. George Osborne sees saving as enabling rather than replacing consumer spending. The coalition government also made a specific link between general, short-term saving and support for the housing market by announcing the 'HTB ISA' in 2015. This measure will offer tax-advantaged saving to those looking to buy a home. Any intention to reduce public spending in this area—a specific rationale for the abolition of the CTF and SG—has again proved to be less influential on policymaking in practice than might have been expected.

Conclusion

The politics of austerity represents perhaps neoliberalism's greatest triumph, in that it has retained its hegemonic status despite the growth model it supports experiencing a profound crisis. It has survived in the UK by moving further towards what Mirowski might understand as monetarist neoliberalism—so much so that the limits of monetary policy have been breached, with monetary activism in the coalition and Conservative governments' economic policy agenda (building to some extent on their predecessor's immediate response to the events of 2008) bleeding into extensive fiscal risks and spending commitments by the state in order to sustain the growth model and the housing market in particular. At the same time, the legitimation of this strategy is very Austrian, with austerity valorising the notion of self-sufficiency within an unalterable marketplace, where state intervention only postpones economic reality, allowing inefficiency and dependency to fester. It is for this reason that fiscal policy now goes by another name. Its demonisation constrains the government's ability to mitigate the crisis effectively, but also serves to undermine the legitimacy of any alternative paths to recovery.

As much as financialisation was part of the causal context of the crisis, it has also proved to be one of its main beneficiaries. The transformation of individual economic practice that financialisation both embodies and demands has, via austerity discourse, come to be seen as the only way for individuals to ensure their security in a harsh economic climate, even if this ultimately entails taking greater rather than fewer risks with our financial well-being. The fiscal consequences of the state helping us to live more ascetically, primarily through home ownership, are obscured by the imaginaries conjured by austerity, irrespective of what they cost. That the economy has finally returned to growth—a rather unremarkable feat—takes on an almost epic significance as the consequence of collective belt-tightening. It is of course the result of the opposite, with greater spending by individuals on housing, and consumer spending enabled to some extent by housing wealth, coupled with what amounts to a comprehensive housing market stimulus package from the Treasury and the Bank of England, playing a decisive role in nudging the statistics in the right direction. The arrangement is unsustainable, because housing bubbles burst. Yet austerity has triumphed in embedding the norms of financialisation in common sense, helping to define the crisis of financialisation as one of not enough financialisation, and obscuring the herculean efforts of policy elites to salvage a process that had been imperilled by the 2008 crash.

Note

1. Data on housing equity withdrawal were downloaded from the Bank of England's statistical interactive database, available at http://www.bankofengland.co.uk/boeapps/iadb/newintermed.asp; data on household consumption were downloaded from the Office for National Statistics Quarterly National Accounts time series dataset, available at http://www.ons.gov.uk/ons/rel/naa2/quarterly-national-accounts/index.html.

References

Allen, K., & Pickard, J. (2015). Help to Buy has pushed up house prices, says study. *Financial Times*, September 20. http://www.ft.com/cms/s/0/fdbb8a00-5dfe-11e5-9846-de406ccb37f2.html#axzz3pqy4GHkF. Accessed 20 Oct 2015.

Bank of England. (2012). *The distributional effects of asset purchases*. http://www.bankofengland.co.uk/publications/Documents/news/2012/nr073.pdf. Accessed 20 Oct 2015.

Bank of England. (2014). *Inflation report: February 2014*. http://www.bankofengland.co.uk/publications/Pages/inflationreport/2014/ir1401.aspx. Accessed 1 Sept 2015.

Berry, C. (2014a). Austerity, ageing and the financialisation of pensions policy in the UK. *British Politics*, November 10. http://dx.doi.org/10.1057/bp.2014.19

Berry, C. (2015). Citizenship in a financialised society: Financial inclusion and the state before and after the crash. *Policy and Politics, 43*(4), 509–525.

Berry, C., & Hay, C. (2014). The great British 'rebalancing' act: The construction and implementation of an economic imperative for exceptional times. *British Journal of Politics and International Relations*, published online 12 December 2014. http://dx.doi.org/10.1111/1467-856X.12063

Berry, C., & Hay, C. (2015). Has the UK economy been 'rebalanced'? Sheffield Political Economy Research Institute British Political Economy Brief no. 14. http://speri.dept.shef.ac.uk/wp-content/uploads/2015/07/Brief14-Has-the-UK-economy-been-rebalanced.pdf. Accessed 20 Oct 2015.

Cameron, D. (2013). Economy speech. Speech delivered on 7 March 2013. https://www.gov.uk/government/speeches/economy-speech-delivered-by-david-cameron. Accessed 20 Oct 2015.

Davies, W. (2014). *The limits to neoliberalism: Authority, sovereignty and the logic of competition*. London: SAGE.

Dolphin, T. (2014). Why the Bank of England should not increase interest rates in 2015. *Left Foot Forward*, December 29. http://leftfootforward.org/2014/12/why-the-bank-of-england-should-not-increase-interest-rates-in-2015/. Accessed 10 Dec 2015.

Forbes, K. (2015). Avoiding sunburn and other considerations for interest rates. *The Telegraph*, August 16. http://www.telegraph.co.uk/finance/bank-of-england/11803024/Kristin-Forbes-Avoiding-sunburn-and-other-considerations-for-interest-rates.html. Accessed 20 Oct 2015.

Gamble, A. (2014). *Crisis without end: The unravelling of Western prosperity.* Basingstoke: Palgrave Macmillan.

Green, J., & Lavery, S. (2015). The regressive recovery: Distribution, inequality and state power in Britain's post-crisis political economy. *New Political Economy*, published online 20 May 2015. http://dx.doi.org/10.1080/13563467.2015.1041478

Joyce, M., Tong, M., & Wood, R. (2011). The United Kingdom's quantitative easing policy: Design, operation and impact. *Bank of England Quarterly Bulletin – Q3.* http://www.bankofengland.co.uk/publications/Documents/quarterlybulletin/qb110301.pdf. Accessed 20 Oct 2015.

Kelly, G. (2013). Britain needs to face up to its household debts. *Financial Times*, December 3. http://www.ft.com/cms/s/0/6227e27a-5b6f-11e3-848e-00144feabdc0.html#axzz3q1xZZTyD. Accessed 20 Oct 2015.

Keynes, J. M. (1919). *The economic consequences of the peace.* London: Macmillan.

Mirowski, P. (2014). *Never let a serious crisis go to waste: How neoliberalism survived the financial meltdown.* London: Verso.

Office for Budget Responsibility. (2011a). *Economic and fiscal outlook: March 2011.* http://budgetresponsibility.org.uk/economic-and-fiscal-outlook-march-2011/. Accessed 20 Oct 2015.

Office for National Statistics. (2014b). *Wealth in Great Britain 2010–12: Total wealth.* http://www.ons.gov.uk/ons/dcp171776_362809.pdf. Accessed 11 Aug 2015.

Osborne, G. (2011). Party conference speech. Speech delivered on 3 October 2011. http://www.telegraph.co.uk/news/politics/georgeosborne/8804027/Conservative-Party-Conference-2011-George-Osborne-speech-in-full.html. Accessed 20 Oct 2015.

Pettifor, A. (2013). "Speech notes for presentation to the Just Banking conference, Edinburgh, 20 April, 2012", *Debtonation*, 27 April. Available from: http://www.debtonation.org/2012/04/ann-pettifor-speech-notes-for-presentation-to-the-just-banking-conference-edinburgh-20th-april-2012-2/. Accessed 20 Oct 2015.

Pickard, J. (2014). Britain's housing benefit bill to rise to £27bn by 2018/19. *The Financial Times*, August 5. http://www.ft.com/cms/s/0/ef999948-1bed-11e4-9666-00144feabdc0.html#axzz3pqy4GHkF. Accessed 20 Oct 2015.

Reuters. (2015). Carney says BoE rate likely to rise, contrasts with Haldane. http://uk.reuters.com/article/2015/03/30/uk-britain-boe-carney-idUKKBN0MN14320150330. Accessed 20 Oct 2015.

CHAPTER 3

Industrial Decline and the Myth of Rebalancing

Abstract The notion that the UK economy needs to be 'rebalanced' has become one of the most important motifs of elite-level public discourse. The most important imbalances to which policy is ostensibly being addressed are those between the finance and manufacturing sectors, and between Northern and Southern England. However, rebalancing does not endorse a critique of either finance-led growth or *laissez-faire* industrial policy. Instead, it serves to further delegitimise the notion of the state as a purposeful economic actor, complementing the master narrative around austerity. Coalition and Conservative industrial policy has failed to reverse the long-running path of decline in UK manufacturing, and the more recent agenda around 'the Northern Powerhouse' represents the transposition of austerity-related notions of self-sufficiency from the individual to the civic level.

Keywords Rebalancing • Industrial policy • Manufacturing • Northern England • Devolution • Austerity

The notion that the UK economy needs to be 'rebalanced' has become one of the most important motifs of elite-level public discourse since the financial crisis, promulgated most vociferously by the coalition and Conservative governments. The concept of rebalancing has typically been

C. Berry, *Austerity Politics and UK Economic Policy*, Building a Sustainable Political Economy: SPERI Research & Policy,
DOI 10.1057/978-1-137-59010-7_3

used to refer to a long list of economic issues, most obviously the contribution of different sectors and different regions to the British economy. But rebalancing is also employed to refer to the trade balance, and the relative importance of saving and investment in contrast to, respectively, private debt and consumption. The previous chapter argued that there has been no substantive transition away from a domestic economy based on finance, debt, and the housing market—and suggested that any signs of 'success' in this regard are expected to be short-lived. This chapter concentrates on the apparent geographical (primarily between Northern England and London/the South East) and sectoral (between finance and manufacturing) imbalances.

Although, as discussed below, the Labour government also utilised the notion of economic rebalancing after 2008, the argument that New Labour had allowed the UK economy to become unbalanced formed one of the key critiques, alongside that of profligacy, of their predecessors in office by leading coalition figures. Rebalancing therefore exposes one of the discursive anomalies, or ironies, of the post-crisis era in the UK; in short, rebalancing renews the long standing discourse around economic 'decline' often indulged by elite actors in the UK since the Second World War. Moreover, the emphasis on promoting manufacturing and Northern England, ahead of finance and the City of London, lends weight to some of the most critical declinist accounts of UK economic statecraft, typified by economic sociologist Geoffrey Ingham (1984) and political economist Karel Williams (Williams et al. 1983). Such accounts of the decline of the UK economy emphasised the role of an excessively large financial sector in attracting labour market talent, investment, and macroeconomic policy support away from sectors such as manufacturing, even though the finance sector was itself incapable of delivering real economic value.

Generally speaking, the process of financialisation means that the problems identified by Ingham and Williams have intensified since the 1980s. Is it possible therefore that the Conservative discourse of rebalancing actually contradicts the mutually beneficial relationship between austerity and financialisation that appears to have been at the heart of the coalition and Conservative governments' economic policy agenda? This chapter argues not. The extent to which the public discourse on rebalancing actually propels economic policymaking in practice can of course be questioned (as with the discourse around austerity). Yet the chapter's principal objection to the possibility that rebalancing contradicts austerity and financialisation by endorsing the notion of a finance-induced decline is that rebalancing discourse actually stops well short of endorsing the view that the UK economy (and the way it is governed), or any of its component sectors, is fundamentally flawed. The industrial and regional policy agenda to which it appears to have given rise offers little threat to the key elements of the pre-crisis growth model. Indeed, parts of this agenda constitute integral elements of the elite politics of austerity, insofar as austerity heralds an adjustment to the aspects of the pre-crisis growth model deemed most problematic, rather than its wholesale replacement. The chapter begins by documenting examples of coalition and Conservative rhetoric on rebalancing, and exploring its relationship with austerity. It then focuses consecutively on the most important dimensions of economic rebalancing, as espoused by policy elites in the post-crisis period: firstly, industrial policy, and secondly, devolution to city-regions.

Rebalancing and Austerity

The notion of economic rebalancing began to feature heavily in the Conservative Party's public discourse in advance of the 2010 election. The party's manifesto promised 'a more balanced economy' (Conservative Party 2010). Immediately after the election, the published agreement between the Conservatives and Liberal Democrats stipulated that creating 'a fairer and more balanced economy, where we are not so dependent on a narrow range of economic sectors, and where new businesses and economic opportunities are more evenly shared between regions and industries', was one of the key coalition priorities (HM Government 2010, p. 9). The highly anticipated 'plan for growth', co-authored between the Conservative-led Treasury and the Liberal Democrat-led Department for Business, Innovation, and Skills (BIS), argued that 'sustainable growth requires a rebalancing of the UK economy away from a reliance on a narrow range of sectors and regions, to one built on investment and exports, with strong growth more fairly shared across the UK' (HM Treasury and BIS 2011, p. 28). David Cameron (2010b) had explicitly referred in a post-election speech to the relationship between finance and London, on the one hand, and manufacturing and the North, on the other: 'our economy has become more and more unbalanced, with our fortunes hitched to a few industries in one corner of the country, while we let other sectors like manufacturing slide'.

This is not to suggest that rebalancing and related concepts were invented by the Conservative Party or the coalition government. As early as 2002, then Governor of the Bank of England, Mervyn King, told the British Chambers of Commerce that 'the need to rebalance the British economy is clear' (King 2002). The term appears to have started to make reasonably frequent appearances in mainstream media commentary on the economy from this point onwards (Berry and Hay 2014, p. 6). King reiterated the argument in giving evidence to the Treasury select committee in 2008, before the collapse of Lehman Brothers (see House of Commons Treasury Committee 2008). After the financial crisis, leading Labour figures also started to employ discourse related to economic rebalancing, including then Chancellor, Alistair Darling (2009), and then Secretary of State for Business, Peter Mandelson, who argued that 'we have allowed ourselves to become over-dependent on the City and financial services for growth and our tax revenues. That is why … we need other industrial strengths and sources of revenue to grow faster' (Mandelson 2010). Although the discourse does not appear to have been used by Ed Miliband in his time as leader of the Labour Party to any significant extent, it was employed by other leading figures within the Labour opposition after 2010, including Chuka Umunna, Rachel Reeves, and Andrew Adonis (who subsequently resigned the Labour whip in the House of Lords to take up a post in the Conservative administration) (The Adonis Review 2014; Reeves 2013; Rigby 2014).

As noted in the previous chapter, the Conservative Party found it increasingly difficult to talk publicly about its approach to personal debt, given the apparent contradiction between austerity and an economic recovery fuelled by debt—this may be one of the reasons that rebalancing discourse quietened within government rhetoric after 2012. The off-message Liberal Democrat business secretary, Vince Cable, used concerns around indebtedness and an overheated housing market as part of the rationale for rebalancing, arguing that the economy 'needs rebalancing through a shift to exports and investment rather than debt-based consumption—specifically towards long-term investment in productive assets rather than short-term speculative property accumulation' (Cable 2013). However, George Osborne's more recent references to rebalancing discourse have seemingly deliberately marginalised concerns around debt. He has argued, somewhat duplicitously, that the recovery witnessed since 2013 is a partial result of the coalition's success in rebalancing the economy, while reiterating the need for higher investment, higher exports, and greater support for manufacturing (Osborne 2014a, b).

Rebalancing clearly plays an important role in the framing of the Conservative Party's economic policy agenda. Yet we can question the extent to which it valorises genuinely significant or meaningful economic change. Clearly, the notion of *re*balancing suggests that there once was balance. While this acknowledges significant economic problems or 'imbalances' (which could hardly not be acknowledged, in the wake of the financial crisis), the discourse handily identifies poor economic management (by someone else) as responsible for disrupting some natural economic balance. While it is possible to restore such balance, rebalancing discourse also conveniently serves even to offer a 'get out of jail free card' to those responsible for this task should growth results underwhelm while the rebalancing project is undertaken. It is also worth considering what the underlying notion of economic balance appears to be telling us about the nature of the problems faced by the economy. The concept suggests that all of the component parts of the existing economic model are legitimate and capable of functioning effectively, but they have simply become disordered. As such, underperforming sectors, such as manufacturing, or regions, such as the Northern regions, can be boosted simply by policymakers deciding to focus their fiscal levers on the sector, and not by focusing on the interplay and interaction between different sectors and regions (Berry 2013; Berry and Hay 2014; Froud et al. 2011; Lee 2015).

The relationship between the concepts of rebalancing and austerity, and associated discourses is rather complex. But recognising the essential conservatism of rebalancing helps us understand their largely mutually beneficial interaction. Insofar as rebalancing implies the existence a priori of (the possibility of) a naturally occurring economic balance, it is not difficult to see how austerity's demonisation of the state, particularly fiscal policy, might be considered a prerequisite of allowing this natural order to reassert itself. Of course, rebalancing discourse quite explicitly advocates action by state actors, but in positioning itself in relation to the ideal of balance, it clearly circumscribes the parameters of state intervention in terms of economic spheres (supporting flailing sectors or regions, not impeding successful ones) and time (rebalancing is a temporary or even one-off initiative) (Berry and Hay 2014, p. 2). This is closely related to the notion that achieving balance would require only minor, technocratic modifications to economic practice, rather than interventions that might hinder market logic (Froud et al. 2011, p. 12). For this reason, the primary fiscal levers pulled by the state are minor tax adjustments (invariably cuts), rather than, say, major public investment programmes or corporate governance reform. As such, rebalancing creates an imperative for inaction as much as it does for action.

Industrial Policy and Manufacturing Since the Crisis

Is the coalition and Conservative governments' rhetoric on supporting manufacturing—and increasingly, the Conservative government's rhetoric on its success in rebalancing the economy towards manufacturing—matched by evidence of improved performance in the UK manufacturing sector? George Osborne (2011a) promised to bring about 'the march of the makers' in 2011, but there is little evidence that he has succeeded. The manufacturing sector in fact now constitutes a *smaller* part of the UK economy than before the financial crisis (9.7 per cent of total output, i.e., gross value added [GVA], at the end of 2014, compared to 10.9 per cent in late 2007); it is worth noting that the finance and insurance sector is a smaller component too (7.4 per cent compared to 9.9 per cent), while services in general have grown to more than four-fifths of UK GVA. However, while jobs in finance and insurance have been largely stable over this period, more than 400,000 jobs were lost in the manufacturing sector between late 2007 and early 2015 (Berry and Hay 2015, p. 2). Output in the manufacturing sector remains more than 6 per cent below its pre-crisis peak in 2007. The only manufacturing industry to have experienced significant output growth over this period is transport equipment (largely car manufacturing).[1]

Even the recent success of UK car manufacturing can be questioned. New production largely consists of Japanese-owned firms increasing production in the UK (ONS 2013). These firms have seemingly been attracted by falling real wages and sterling's significant depreciation; that so few other industries have benefitted from the same dynamic is quite remarkable, and demonstrates a significant dearth of capacity in most manufacturing industries (Berry 2014d). Moreover, while in Germany 60 per cent of the content of cars assembled is actually manufactured in Germany, in the UK only around a third of the components of cars assembled are produced within the country (Stewart 2013). Strong domestic demand for cars is also part of the explanation for car manufacturing's relative success, but this demand may not persist; *The Guardian* reported in early 2014 on the rather ironic role being played by Payment Protection Insurance compensation (a product of mis-selling in the UK banking sector) in supporting this demand (Monaghan 2014). The continuing struggles of the manufacturing sector help to explain the coalition and Conservative governments' poor record on addressing UK productivity (ONS 2015c), which George Osborne acknowledged recently, and rather belatedly, as 'the challenge of our time' (cited in Dathan 2015). UK policy elites have consistently underestimated the role of manufacturing in propelling productivity growth throughout the economy (Chang 2014, pp. 258–262). It also helps to explain the persistence of the UK's enormous balance of payments deficit, with a current account deficit of £17.5 billion (including a trade deficit of £8.7 billion) recorded in late 2015 (ONS 2015a). Although the trade deficit was highlighted in early Conservative rhetoric on rebalancing, in general the balance of payments has barely featured in mainstream media coverage of the coalition and Conservative governments' economic performance.

Of course, the performance of manufacturing since the financial crisis should not be crudely associated with the crisis itself, or indeed solely with a flawed response to the crisis by the coalition and Conservative governments. It signifies more generally the continuation, and possibly intensification (although the trends may yet stabilise), of a longer-term decline in UK manufacturing. Firstly, it must be noted that manufacturing had not shared in the pre-crisis boom. There had been no upturn in manufacturing output between 2002 and 2007 (Froud et al. 2011, pp. 26–28). Secondly, manufacturing in the UK has been in relative decline throughout the post-war period. Output in the sector has grown significantly less strongly than those in other Organisation for Economic Co-operation and Development (OECD) countries (Matthews 2007, pp. 766–771). More than 2 million jobs were lost in the manufacturing sector during the 1980s, with almost 1 million more under the Major government in the 1990s, and around 1.5 million under the Blair and Brown governments (Froud et al. 2011, p. 18). The globalisation of production, networks evident over this period, offers only a partial explanation for this trend. Global manufacturing may have become more international in character from the 1970s onwards, but non-OECD countries have not, as a whole, seen increases in either the number of people employed in manufacturing, or the proportion of the world's manufacturing workforce located within their borders. It is true that the UK lost many low-skilled manufacturing jobs to developing countries over this period, but also many high-skilled jobs to OECD rivals (Pilat et al. 2006).

The coalition and Conservative governments have made few substantive efforts to address long-term manufacturing decline. Contemporary industrial policy reflects both the limited and technocratic policy agenda surreptitiously endorsed by the rebalancing agenda and, more pertinently, long standing industrial policy traditions in the UK. Industrial policy is generally not focused on manufacturing in particular, but rather typically takes the form of initiatives to support regional development or small- and medium-sized enterprises (SMEs) or forms of 'soft' support such as tax allowances or advisory services (Buigues and Sekkat 2009). If the coalition and Conservative approach to industrial policy can be considered a departure from tradition to any extent, its novelty probably lies in its endorsement of 'advanced manufacturing'—yet probably insofar as this signifies a willingness to overlook manufacturing in general, rather than any particularly substantive (rather than rhetorical) reorientation towards high-value manufacturing industries or activities. The Treasury/BIS plan for growth exalted advanced manufacturing, but offered only moderate policy changes, including extending tax allowances, establishing more extensive forms of advice and dissemination networks, some additional support for relevant university-based research centres, and a small amount of investment in new apprenticeship schemes (HMT and BIS 2011). More specific forms of support, including reasonably significant direct investment by government, was established in 2010 through the Advanced Manufacturing Supply Chain Initiative, led by Vince Cable at BIS. Such initiatives fall well short of the new industrial policy partnership between government and the private sector envisaged by Michael Heseltine's *No Stone Unturned* review, published in 2013 (commissioned by George Osborne, although not necessarily enthusiastically), yet Heseltine made relatively few specific references to how manufacturing in particular could be supported (Heseltine 2013). Of course, the advanced manufacturing agenda is not entirely new, even in terms of the short period since the financial crisis, given that the Labour government's support for rebalancing after 2008 manifests most strongly in a renewed focus on supporting advanced manufacturing through what Peter Mandelson called 'a new industrial activism' (cited in Stratton 2008).

The most obvious critique of the coalition and Conservative governments' support for advanced manufacturing is that it has not been associated with a significant increase in public investment in areas that might nurture higher value-added manufacturing capacity; even efforts to enable higher levels of private investment in this regard have focused on 'nudging' private investors towards favoured projects rather than considering the structural barriers to allocating capital to improving the productive capacity of the UK economy over the long term (Berry 2014b). We can also point to George Osborne's recent embrace of China as evidence of the Conservative government's unwillingness to provide or facilitate higher native investment. The government has resisted demands to establish a national investment bank, along the lines of Germany's KfW; they established the Green Investment Bank (GIB) with a small amount of public investment in order to fund projects that support environmentally sustainable production, but privatised the GIB in 2015—before it actually began to function as a bank. George Osborne has also begun the process of privatising, at a loss, the Royal Bank of Scotland and the Lloyds Banking Group (part of an unprecedented sell-off of public assets, which also included the Royal Mail, on Vince Cable's watch), without taking the opportunity to fundamentally reshape their lending practices. However, the Centre for Research on Socio-Cultural Change (CRESC)—led by Karel Williams—has strongly criticised the apparent consensus around supporting advanced manufacturing, including where supported by groups ostensibly on the left such as trade unions. For CRESC, the agenda to support advanced manufacturing, even were it to involve substantial public investment as trade unions have advocated, distinguishes too crudely between low- and high-tech manufacturing and overlooks too quickly the possibility that structural defects within UK manufacturing (rather than simply exogenous constraints, such as a lack of skilled workers) are prohibiting the growth of advanced manufacturing industries (Bentham et al. 2013). Predictably, despite much fanfare, there is little or no evidence that the UK has caught up, to any extent, with other advanced economies in advanced manufacturing industries since the financial crisis.

Powerhouse Politics

The Conservative majority government's Northern Powerhouse agenda—strongly associated with George Osborne (2015)—suggests that it is far more focused on geographical rather than sectoral rebalancing than the coalition government was. It is perhaps telling that the advanced manufacturing agenda barely featured in the Treasury's so-called productivity plan, published in 2015 (HM Treasury 2015). This shift was foretold, to some extent, by *No Stone Unturned*, which focused far more on the subnational delivery mechanisms for a new industrial strategy, rather than the content of what they might actually deliver. Of course, it also signifies a return to the traditional conflation of regional and industrial policy or, more precisely, substitution of regional policy for industrial policy. The Conservative Party's newfound interest in regional development in England was partly inspired by events in Scotland, with David Cameron having promised greater devolution throughout the UK in the wake of a very narrow result in favour of Scotland remaining in the union. As such, there is a constitutional as well as an industrial policy dimension to the Northern Powerhouse agenda. However, it certainly appears that the constitutional issues are a distant second to economic issues in terms of Northern England. Although Osborne has made the establishment of directly elected, city-region mayors for combined authorities a core part of the Northern Powerhouse agenda, this objective has generally proceeded with very little public consultation (indeed, some of the areas that will now be covered by mayors rejected similar proposals for directly elected, single-authority mayors in 2012), and the Conservatives have shown greatest appetite for reshaping the constitutional status of England within the Westminster model, rather than its constituent regions (Kenny 2014). It is important to note that although the Northern Powerhouse agenda surfaced most strongly towards the end of the life of the coalition, and then after the 2015 general election, this does not mean that the Liberal Democrats had, in government, sought to hold back the thrust of devolution in Northern England. Arguably, Nick Clegg's Northern Futures initiative, orchestrated through the Cabinet Office, was an important forerunner to Northern Powerhouse and exhibited a greater willingness to treat the constitutional status of Northern cities and regions, and their economic prospects, as equally important dilemmas (Clegg 2014).

The meat on the bones of the Northern Powerhouse is the series of devolution deals signed between central government and combined authorities (whether existing or newly combined)—and such deals are of course not exclusive to Northern cities and regions. However, the powers being devolved are rather limited. Although not every city-region will have the same array of powers devolved (and there are variations based on the new local governance arrangements chosen), there are some common features. Some powers over transport will be devolved, although generally not powers to decide on major infrastructure projects. Some planning powers will be devolved, alongside housing investment budgets. Some aspects of central government's skills and employment support powers will be devolved, including further education and apprenticeships. Local authorities or mayors will also now have greater scope to co-commission Work Programme services (the government's flagship welfare-to-work scheme, discussed in the next chapter). Generally, the majority of business support initiatives, including manufacturing advisory services, will be devolved to the local level. None of this amounts to what would be considered industrial policy in a continental European context—because the UK has little by way of industrial policy to devolve, and limited BIS budgets for direct investment in productive capacity will remain exactly where they are, for the most part. There will seemingly be no reinstatement of the investment budgets that the coalition government closed when they abolished the Labour government's flagship Regional Development Agencies in favour of Local Enterprise Partnerships (LEPs), which aim to co-ordinate rather than fund local development initiatives (and may become defunct as devolution unfolds). Elements of the Conservative Party's devolution agenda hint at a centralising as well as localising objective. The expectation that directly elected mayors will be established is the best example. Furthermore, in the midst of ongoing negotiations between the Treasury and local authorities, George Osborne announced the wholesale devolution of business rates (a tax on the physical footprint of private companies), which is expected to enable city-regions to collect and spend business rates revenue as they see fit. However, he also announced that local authorities would not actually be able to raise the level of business rates in their area, only cut it (unless the private sector appointees on the relevant LEP board agree to a capped surcharge to fund local infrastructure project) (HM Treasury 2015a).

Such policies further suggest that Northern cities and regions will not be empowered to pursue economic policy agendas which differ fundamentally from that favoured by central government under the stewardship of the Conservative Party, and that the underlying objective of the Northern Powerhouse agenda is to complement central government's efforts to make the UK attractive to exogenous investment. Moreover, city-regions in the North might be expected to compete to make their areas more attractive than rival areas, a logic which lends itself to the Conservative Party's agenda around reducing levels of taxation on private sector activity and creates the possibility that while some parts of the North will find ways to increase prosperity as a result of devolution in the form on offer, some may fall further behind London and the South East.

Even the terminology of the North as a 'powerhouse'—ironically playing upon its industrial heritage—appears to circumscribe the role expected of Northern city-regions in supporting the UK in the 'global race'. The Conservative government appears to be implying that their devolution agenda liberates an existing economic powerhouse, thereby marginalising the possibility that peripheral regions in England might be structurally disadvantaged.

The Northern Powerhouse agenda has advanced within two crucial contexts. Firstly, the apparent failure of economic rebalancing since 2010: at the end of 2013 (the latest data available), output in each of the three Northern regions represented a smaller proportion of overall UK output than before the financial crisis, while London and the wider South East both represent higher proportions. Similarly, while output per head has fallen across the North over this period, it has risen in London and the South East (Berry and Hay 2015, pp. 2, 3). The second context is the relationship between devolution and austerity. It is clearly not coincidental that the Conservative Party have begun to consider how to, ostensibly, support economic development in Northern England, as their austerity agenda begins to decimate the role of the public sector in supporting employment and consumption in the North—perhaps the most significant element of the pre-crisis growth model that UK policy elites have *not* sought to maintain in the post-crisis period. In fact, there is significant evidence that public sector employment and investment cuts have fallen more heavily on the Northern regions than elsewhere (Berry et al. 2015; Lavery 2015). The North is being asked to become more self-sufficient (a prescription based on the dubious diagnosis—albeit one consistent with the idea of austerity—that the North had previously been dependent on more prosperous parts of the UK). Indeed, Osborne's decision regarding the localisation of business rates came alongside the suggestion that central government grants to local authorities would be phased out accordingly, a move which would further exacerbate inequalities between England's constituent regions.

The future of fiscal policy within more devolved governance arrangements will almost certainly become a key terrain for Conservative statecraft for the foreseeable future—although the party's agenda in this regard in presently unknown (or undetermined), the controversial move to allow the Greater Manchester combined authority full control over National Health Service (NHS) services within its region (HM Treasury and Greater Manchester Combined Authority 2015) appears to enable central government to relieve itself of certain core functions, so that its own ability to borrow is strengthened. There is an important political dimension to the Northern Powerhouse agenda too. The argument that devolution represents an attempt by Osborne to 'shift the blame' for public spending cuts to the local authorities that will now have to implement them is not entirely without merit, but probably too crude: local authorities can easily make the argument to local voters that their hands are tied, and the existence of directly elected mayors will strengthen their ability to confront central government in this regard. However, it seems likely that the Conservative Party is actually hopeful that they will be able to capture some of the mayoral offices that will be established in Northern city-regions, based on the experience of a directly elected London mayor that the candidate's personality can be just as important as their party affiliation in gaining support in electoral contests of this nature. It is also the case that the character of the powers that will be possessed by mayors lends itself to a pro-business political narrative, which sits more comfortably within a Conservative lexicon. As such, the Northern Powerhouse agenda is motivated, at least to some extent, by the possibility of disrupting one of the long standing sources of political power for the Labour Party. This is not to suggest that the Northern Powerhouse agenda should be seen as an Osborne 'divide and conquer' masterplan (it was described as a 'cruel deception' by Jeremy Corbyn (2015a) during the 2015 Labour leadership election). While rescuing the core elements of the pre-crisis growth model, within which the Northern regions were largely subservient, is the Conservative government's agenda, and considerations of political strategy are certainly part of the Conservatives' thinking, the agenda could equally be seen as indication of the difficulty that elites face in maintaining the pre-crisis growth model in a post-crisis environment. Devolution will certainly not be as effective as public sector investment proved to be in minimising concerns around geographical inequalities in the UK (especially once devolved budgets are further eroded from the centre). Moreover, the agenda offers an ideological platform—if not quite yet the policy levers—to challenge austerity from the North.

Conclusion

It would be far too cynical to conclude that the Conservative Party accepts the ongoing decline of manufacturing in the UK—the main, underlying cause of the UK's productivity problem—or the lower levels of prosperity that remain evident in England's Northern regions. Their policy agenda may ultimately shower a significant degree of support for the London-based finance sector, as the central element of the growth model they remain wedded to, but this does not mean that they are entirely indifferent to other sectors and regions. However, it is fair to say that the coalition and Conservative governments have not recognised these problems as evidence of decline and have therefore not formed policy programmes around the objective of arresting industrial decline. Policy elites in the UK became comfortable after 2008 with describing the UK economy as unbalanced, but not with acknowledging that it has profound, structural flaws. If the economy was unbalanced in the period leading up to the financial crisis, by definition it must have been balanced—and therefore fundamentally sound—at some point in the relatively recent past.

Both of the policy areas discussed in this chapter indicate that the coalition and Conservative governments have not been prepared to substantially alter the key precepts of pre-crisis economic statecraft in order to restore balance to the UK economy. The coalition's renewed focus on advanced manufacturing—taking forward its predecessor's agenda to some extent—fuelled much fanfare about 'the march of the makers', but clearly signalled the government's reluctance to support UK manufacturing in general. Similarly, the Northern Powerhouse agenda offers moral support to the England's struggling Northern regions, but tells them ultimately that they are now required to look after themselves. Nevertheless, both agendas lend credibility to the argument that the pre-crisis growth cannot simply be dusted down and fired up again—their existence heralds at least some possibility of meaningful economic policy change. Of course, the overriding logic of austerity discourse plays a crucial role in mitigating this possibility, to the extent that discourses around industrial policy and devolution may even be helping to reinforce the worldview promulgated by the austerity concept. As such, like rebalancing discourse in general, they may be helping to legitimise the pre-crisis growth model even as they offer a critique of pre-crisis economic organisation. Advanced manufacturing and the North should be supported, but only because the UK finds itself contesting a race for globally mobile investment. Too much support in the form of state intervention would therefore be counterproductive to the development of lean and competitive high-tech industries in the Northern regions.

Note

1. Data on the performances of manufacturing industries were downloaded from the Office for National Statistics Index of Production time series dataset, available at http://www.ons.gov.uk/ons/rel/iop/index-of-production/index.html.

References

Bentham, J., Bowman, A., Froud, J., Johal, S., Leaver, A., & Williams, K. (2013). Against new industrial strategy: Framings, motifs and absences. CRESC working paper no. 126. http://www.cresc.ac.uk/medialibrary/workingpapers/wp126.pdf. Accessed 12 Aug 2015.

Berry, C. (2013). Are we there yet? Growth, rebalancing and the pseudo-recovery. Sheffield Political Economy Research Institute paper no. 7. http://speri.dept.shef.ac.uk/wp-content/uploads/2013/01/SPERI-Paper-No.7-Are-We-There-Yet-PDF-747KB.pdf. Accessed 31 Jul 2015.

Berry, C. (2014b, November 4). Pension funds and the city in the UK's contradictory growth spurts. Paper presented at *Capital divided? The City of London and the future of the British economy*, City University London. https://www.academia.edu/9094932/Pension_funds_and_the_City_in_the_UKs_contradictory_growth_spurts. Accessed 9 Nov 2014.

Berry, C. (2014d). Sterling depreciation and the UK trade balance. Sheffield Political Economy Research Institute British Political Economy Brief no. 2. http://speri.dept.shef.ac.uk/wp-content/uploads/2014/01/SPERI-British-Political-Economy-Brief-No.2-%E2%80%93-Sterling-depreciation-the-UK-trade-balance.pdf. Accessed 9 Nov 2014.

Berry, C., & Hay, C. (2014). The great British 'rebalancing' act: The construction and implementation of an economic imperative for exceptional times. *British Journal of Politics and International Relations*, published online 12 December 2014. http://dx.doi.org/10.1111/1467-856X.12063

Berry, C., & Hay, C. (2015). Has the UK economy been 'rebalanced'? Sheffield Political Economy Research Institute British Political Economy Brief no. 14. http://speri.dept.shef.ac.uk/wp-content/uploads/2015/07/Brief14-Has-the-UK-economy-been-rebalanced.pdf. Accessed 20 Oct 2015.

Berry, C., Hunt, T., & White, L. (2015). Public infrastructure investment and business activity in the English regions. Sheffield Political Economy Research Institute British Political Economy Brief no. 15. http://speri.dept.shef.ac.uk/wp-content/uploads/2015/08/SPERI-Brief-No.15-Public-infrastructure-investment-business-activity-in-the-English-regions.pdf. Accessed 8 Nov 2015.

Buigues, P.-A. & Sekkat, K. (2009). *Industrial Policy in Europe, Japan and the United States: Amounts, Mechanisms and Effectiveness*. Basingstoke: Palgrave Macmillan.

Cable, V. (2013). Speech to the industrial strategy conference 2013. Speech delivered on 11 September 2013. https://www.gov.uk/government/speeches/industrial-strategy-conference-2013. Accessed 2 Aug 2015.

Cameron, D. (2010b). Transforming the British economy: Coalition strategy for economic growth. Speech delivered on 28 May 2010. https://www.gov.uk/government/speeches/transforming-the-british-economy-coalition-strategy-for-economic-growth. Accessed 9 Nov 2015.

Chang, H.-J. (2014). *Economics: The user's guide*. London: Pelican.

Clegg, N. (2014). Speech at Northern Futures Summit. Speech delivered on 6 November 2014. https://www.gov.uk/government/speeches/nick-clegg-at-northern-futures-summit. Accessed 8 Nov 2015.

Corbyn, J. (2015a). *Northern future*. https://d3n8a8pro7vhmx.cloudfront.net/jeremyforlabour/pages/103/attachments/original/1438626641/NorthernFuture.pdf?1438626641. Accessed 8 Nov 2015.

Darling, A. (2009). Budget speech. Speech delivered on 22 April 2009. http://www.theguardian.com/uk/2009/apr/22/budget-2009-alistair-darling-speech. Accessed 9 Nov 2015.

Dathan, M. (2015). Three charts that show how poor productivity is in the UK – But is it because we're just lazy? *The Independent*, July 10. http://www.independent.co.uk/news/uk/politics/three-charts-that-show-how-poor-productivity-is-in-the-uk-but-is-it-because-we-re-just-lazy-10380200.html. Accessed 1 Nov 2015.

Froud, J., Johal, S., Law, J., Leaver, A., & Williams, K. (2011). Rebalancing the economy (or buyer's remorse). CRESC working paper no. 87. http://www.cresc.ac.uk/publications/rebalancing-the-economy-or-buyers-remorse. Accessed 28 Feb 2014.

Heseltine, M. (2013). *No stone unturned in the pursuit of growth*. https://www.gov.uk/government/uploads/system/uploads/attachment_data/file/34648/12-1213-no-stone-unturned-in-pursuit-of-growth.pdf. Accessed 1 Nov 2015.

HM Government. (2010). *The coalition: Our programme for government*. https://www.gov.uk/government/uploads/system/uploads/attachment_data/file/78977/coalition_programme_for_government.pdf. Accessed 9 Nov 2015.

HM Treasury. (2015). *Fixing the foundations: Creating a more prosperous nation*. https://www.gov.uk/government/uploads/system/uploads/attachment_data/file/443898/Productivity_Plan_web.pdf. Accessed 8 Nov 2015.

HM Treasury. (2015a). Chancellor unveils 'devolution revolution'. Press release issued on 5 October 2015. https://www.gov.uk/government/news/chancellor-unveils-devolution-revolution. Accessed 8 Nov 2015.

HM Treasury and Department for Business, Innovation and Skills. (2011). *The plan for growth*. https://www.gov.uk/government/publications/plan-for-growth--5. Accessed 1 Nov 2015.

HM Treasury and Greater Manchester Combined Authority. (2015). *Further devolution to the Greater Manchester Combined Authority and directly-elected mayor*. https://www.gov.uk/government/uploads/system/uploads/attachment_data/file/443087/Greater_Manchester_Further_Devolution.pdf. Accessed 8 Nov 2015.

House of Commons Treasury Committee. (2008). *Re-appointment of Mervyn King as Governor of the Bank of England: Volume II, oral and written evidence*. http://www.publications.parliament.uk/pa/cm200708/cmselect/cmtreasy/524/524ii.pdf. Accessed 2 Nov 2015.

Ingham, G. (1984). *Capitalism divided? The city and industry in British social development*. London: Macmillan.

Kenny, M. (2014). The conservatives and EVEL: Where's the spirit of Edmund Burke. *Conservative Home*, November 14. http://www.conservativehome.com/platform/2014/11/michael-kenny-the-conservatives-and-evel-wheres-the-spirit-of-edmund-burke.html. Accessed 8 Nov 2015.

King, M. (2002). Rebalancing the United Kingdom's economy. Speech delivered on 23 April 2002. http://www.bis.org/review/r020423c.pdf. Accessed 9 Nov 2015.

Lavery, S. (2015). Public and private sector employment across the UK since the financial crisis. Sheffield Political Economy Research Institute British Political Economy Brief no. 10. http://speri.dept.shef.ac.uk/wp-content/uploads/2015/02/Brief10-public-sector-employment-across-UK-since-financial-crisis.pdf. Accessed 8 Nov 2015.

Lee, S. (2015). Indebted and unbalanced: The political economy of the coalition. In M. Beech & S. Lee (Eds.), *The Conservative-Liberal coalition: Examining the Cameron-Clegg government* (pp. 16–35). Basingstoke: Palgrave Macmillan.

Mandelson, P. (2010). Going for growth: Building Britain's future economy. Speech delivered on 6 January 2010. http://www.theworkfoundation.com/assets/docs/peter%20mandelson%20speech.pdf. Accessed 9 Nov 2015.

Matthews, D. (2007). The performance of British manufacturing in the post-war long boom. *Business History, 49*(6), 763–779.

Monaghan, A. (2014). UK car sales at highest since onset of the crisis. *The Guardian*, January 7. http://www.theguardian.com/business/2014/jan/07/uk-car-sales-five-year-high-smmt. Accessed 28 Feb 2014.

Office for National Statistics. (2013). *Economic review: October 2013*. http://www.ons.gov.uk/ons/rel/elmr/economic-review/october-2013/art-octoberer.html. Accessed 28 Feb 2014.

Office for National Statistics. (2015a). *Balance of payments: Q3, 2015*. http://www.ons.gov.uk/ons/dcp171778_429314.pdf. Accessed 6 Jan 2016.

Office for National Statistics. (2015c). *International comparisons of productivity*. http://www.ons.gov.uk/ons/rel/icp/international-comparisons-of-productivity/2013---final-estimates/info-icp-feb-15.html. Accessed 9 Nov 2015.

Osborne, G. (2011a). Budget speech. Speech delivered on 23 March 2011. http://webarchive.nationalarchives.gov.uk/20121015000000/http://www.direct.gov.uk/prod_consum_dg/groups/dg_digitalassets/@dg/@en/documents/digitalasset/dg_196028.pdf. Accessed 8 Nov 2015.

Osborne, G. (2014a). Budget speech. Speech delivered on 21 March 2014. http://www.theguardian.com/uk/2012/mar/21/budget-speech-2012-full-text. Accessed on 9 Nov 2015.

Osborne, G. (2014b). Economy speech in Hong Kong. Speech delivered on 20 February 2014. https://www.gov.uk/government/speeches/chancellors-economy-speech-in-hong-kong. Accessed 9 Nov 2015.

Osborne, G. (2015). Speech on building a Northern Powerhouse. https://www.gov.uk/government/speeches/chancellor-on-building-a-northern-powerhouse. Accessed 8 Nov 2015.

Pilat, D., Cimper, A., Olsen, K., & Webb, C. (2006). The changing nature of manufacturing in OECD countries. *Organisation for Economic Co-operation and Development.* STI working paper 2006/9. http://www.oecd.org/science/inno/37607831.pdf. Accessed 28 Feb 2014.

Reeves, R. (2013). Speech to the IPPR on the Northern economy, speech delivered on 28 January. http://www.rachelreevesmp.co.uk/rachel_s_speech_to_the_ippr_on_the_northern_economy. Accessed 2 Nov 2015.

Rigby, E. (2014). Chuka Umunna says UK economic rebalancing 'mired in chaos'. *FinancialTimes*,August19.http://www.ft.com/cms/s/0/679d7aea-27b5-11e4-b7a9-00144feabdc0.html#axzz3qQjkJGKn. Accessed 2 Nov 2015.

Stewart, H. (2013, 2 December). Carmakers' success does not herald British industrial renaissance. *The Guardian*, December 2. http://www.theguardian.com/business/2013/dec/02/carmarkers-success-not-herald-industrial-revival. Accessed 20 Dec 2015.

Stratton, A. (2008). Mandelson calls for 'industrial activism' to revitalise Britain after the recession. *The Guardian*, December 3. http://www.theguardian.com/politics/2008/dec/03/peter-mandelson-hugo-young-lecture. Accessed 1 Nov 2015.

The Adonis Review. (2014). *Mending the fractured economy, Policy Network.* http://www.policy-network.net/publications/4695/Mending-the-Fractured-Economy. Accessed 1 Nov 2015.

The Conservative Party. (2010). *An invitation to join the government of Britain: The conservative manifesto 2010.* http://media.conservatives.s3.amazonaws.com/manifesto/cpmanifesto2010_lowres.pdf. Accessed 9 Nov 2015.

Williams, K., Williams, J., & Thomas, D. (1983). *Why are the British bad at manufacturing?* London: Routledge & Kegan Paul.

CHAPTER 4

Welfare Retrenchment and the Perversion of Full Employment

Abstract Paradoxically, while the 'retrenchment' of welfare entitlements has been central to the pursuit of austerity under the Conservative and coalition governments, reducing actual expenditure on social security benefits has not. This is principally explained by the relationship between labour market outcomes and benefit expenditure. Welfare 'retrenchment', in combination with benefit sanctions and employment support programmes, helps to reinforce the notion that individuals must become self-sufficient through work—enabling a disingenuous championing of full employment by Conservative politicians—but does not necessarily lead to significantly lower spending in the short term. However, the valorisation of work occasioned by austerity has helped the government to resurrect the pre-crisis growth model by placing downward pressure on pay and conditions in key growth industries in the services sector.

Keywords Welfare retrenchment • Labour market • Austerity • Active labour market policy • Social security • Full employment

Cuts to social security expenditure are what most people in the UK would think of as the core feature of austerity. Indeed, the impact of austerity in this regard has inspired some outstanding examples of long-form journalism

C. Berry, *Austerity Politics and UK Economic Policy*, Building a Sustainable Political Economy: SPERI Research & Policy,
DOI 10.1057/978-1-137-59010-7_4

and embedded ethnography in recent years, namely Lisa McKenzie's *Getting By: Estates, Class and Culture in Austerity Britain* and Mary O'Hara's *Austerity Bites: A Journey to the Sharp End of the Cuts in the UK*. O'Hara spent a year visiting deprived communities throughout the UK between 2012 and 2013 to document 'how people were experiencing austerity on the ground' (2015, p. 11). In contrast, McKenzie (2015) documents the impact on a single neighbourhood in Nottingham, focusing on the impact of post-2010 policies, but reflecting also on her personal experience of the neighbourhood's problems over a longer period of time. Yet we can question the significance of the role being played by benefit cuts in shaping the real-life experiences that O'Hara and McKenzie document. For both, it is clear that 'the age of austerity' is not one simply characterised by the removal of a social security safety net that had once mitigated the worst implications of poverty. It is a story too of cuts in other parts of public expenditure, in areas such as social care and local transport services, exacerbating everyday problems related to class- and place-based deprivation. But it is also a story of low pay and job insecurity for those that are in work, higher costs of living (most notably housing), and a reliance on high-cost credit to 'make ends meet'. Does the notion of austerity adequately capture the genesis of these problems? Is it right to locate their origins in the establishment of the coalition government in 2010, or perhaps the preceding recession?

A similar study by journalist Tom Clark (2015) (in collaboration with social scientists at the University of Manchester and Harvard University) largely eschews the term austerity, choosing instead to label the present moment as simply 'hard times'. Alongside masses of statistical support, Clark's book details how economic insecurity is experienced by the worst off in society, with reference to cuts in benefit income, but also evidence of levels of happiness and well-being, the changing nature of work, intergenerational conflict, and declining social mobility. It starts from the premise that the 2008 crisis and of course subsequent elite policy responses have exacerbated deep-rooted social problems that were already evident. This approach begs the question, however, of the status that should be afforded to austerity in the designation of our era or, more importantly, in causing the intensification of the existing problems that Clark expertly documents. Are we merely quibbling over semantics? This chapter argues not. While some of the cuts to benefits that have taken place since 2010 have been devastating, they have been neither the core feature of the austerity agenda, nor the principal cause of recent hardships for the poorest groups. However, the wider definition of austerity advanced throughout this book, which includes the instillation of the norm of self-sufficiency at the individual level, is certainly something that has propelled recent developments in social policy, and which increasingly serves to define the way that the worst off are expected to live.

In short, even if the welfare state has not (yet) been significantly *withdrawn*, this does not mean that it has not been successfully *retrenched*. Elite-level actors have seemingly triumphed in laying down a marker which—although such things can never be entirely fixed—clearly signifies which types of risks and hardships warrant mitigation through collectivist mechanisms, and which do not. Welfare retrenchment is not new, but the notion of austerity allows it to be presented as new, with the pre-crisis era presented accordingly as one of excessive welfarism. This chapter begins by firmly placing the welfare retrenchment agenda in the context of labour market restructuring, which enables it to question the link between rising employment and economic recovery. It then looks in more detail at the coalition and Conservative government's agenda on welfare-to-work and 'active labour market policy', and then their approach to cutting social security expenditure.

Employment Growth and Economic Recovery

That unemployment was 'a price worth paying' for maintaining low inflation, as then Chancellor Norman Lamont famously said in 1991, was part of the common sense of UK economic statecraft for most of the 1980s and 1990s, with a Keynesian commitment to full employment in the post-war era having been associated with high inflation, and ultimately 'stagflation' in the 1970s. George Osborne was therefore knowingly borrowing from the left's political lexicon—seemingly one of his favourite pastimes—when he declared in 2014 that he was committed to achieving full employment (Watt and Mason 2014). Of course, as discussed below, the rhetorical commitment was not accompanied by a fundamental 'change of heart' in terms of how employment can be maximised by economic policymakers. Rather, the change of tone reflects the acknowledgement that the costs apparently associated with pursuing full employment are no longer as significant as they had been 20–30 years earlier, due to structural changes within the UK labour market. Inflation is not presently a significant fear—even if, as discussed in the second chapter, it is sometimes still treated as a *potential* threat by monetary policymakers—and many industries in the services sector are labour-intense, meaning controlling the labour supply can be detrimental to business growth. Furthermore, there are now significant human costs associated with *not* seeking to maximise employment, insofar as the Conservative Party's renewed agenda around welfare retrenchment increases the hardship at the individual level resulting, other things being equal, from worklessness.

It is certainly the case that the UK has an enviable record in terms of increasing employment or, perhaps more pertinently, maintaining a high employment rate despite recessionary conditions. Its employment rate for people aged 20–64 was above 76 per cent at the end of 2014, second only to Germany among large European economies, and higher than its pre-crisis peak. The UK's unemployment rate was around 6 per cent; only Germany, Austria, and Luxembourg, whose economies were relatively unharmed in a direct way by the 2008 financial crisis, have lower unemployment among European Union members.[1] Yet there are of course other signals emanating from the UK labour market that offer greater cause for concern. Firstly, as noted in earlier chapters, earnings continue to stagnate. Average weekly earnings in late 2015 remain around 6 per cent below their pre-crisis peak in real terms (in early 2008). This means that they have risen below the rate of inflation—yet it would be wrong to assume that high inflation accounts for this trend, and that earnings will eventually catch up. Indeed, earnings have recently begun to rise again, after sinking to 8 per cent below the pre-crisis peak in early 2014, yet this is principally only because low inflation has now turned into persistent deflation.[2] Secondly, as noted in the previous chapter, productivity in the UK continues to lag significantly behind most other similar economies. Productivity per hour remains below its pre-crisis peak: there are more of us going out to work, but we are producing less when we get there.[3]

Of course, both stagnating pay and stagnating productivity could be thought of as temporary by-products of the coalition and Conservative governments' success in increasing employment. Yet a greater understanding of how higher employment has been operationalised suggests that lower pay and lower productivity may become more permanent features of the UK labour market. There has been a rise in temporary employment (from around 5.5 per cent of the workforce before the crisis to around 6.5 per cent in 2015). Of greater significance, however, is the diffusion of insecurity throughout the labour market. Firstly, there has been a sharp rise in the number of people on 'zero hours' contracts, that is, jobs—which may be permanent or temporary—that do not actually guarantee the employee any work, and therefore pay. There were fewer than 150,000 employees with zero hours contracts in 2008, but almost 750,000 by mid-2015 (ONS 2015b). Secondly, a significant proportion of the increase in employment can be accounted for by self-employment. Since the peak of the recession, around three-quarters of additional people in employment have been self-employed, although growth in the number of employees has begun to outpace growth in the number of self-employees since 2010, albeit far less than would normally be expected. Although people in self-employment typically earn more on average than people in employment, the median self-employee earns less than the median employee, and median earnings for those in self-employment have fallen by 22 per cent since the recession and have continued to fall since 2010. This is partly related to the fact that self-employment is now far less dominated by men than before the crisis, with male self-employees in construction being matched by female self-employees in the lower-paid social care industry (ONS 2014a). The coalition and Conservative governments' labour market success can also be questioned with reference to the distribution of employment opportunities by age, nationality, and region. Employment growth has been concentrated in older age groups (associated with the rise in self-employment). While the employment rate for those aged 18–24 has yet to return to its pre-crisis peak, and for those aged 25–34 it is now only slightly above, it is around 4 percentage points above for those aged 50–64. For those aged 65 and above, there was no recessionary dip—their employment rate has been rising steadily since 2000. A significant increase in immigration after 2012 also tempers the Conservative record on employment; a very high proportion of those entering work since early 2012 have been non-UK nationals.[4] The employment rate has also risen far more in London than anywhere else in the UK—it has actually fallen in the North East, and Yorkshire and Humberside (Berry and Hay 2015, pp. 2, 3). As such, the coalition and Conservative governments' success in terms of employment must be tempered by an acknowledgement that some groups are being left further behind within the labour market.

It is in this context that we can not only challenge the notion that employment growth demonstrates the success of the Conservatives' economic strategy, but also begin to understand its failure in terms of pay and productivity. As noted in the previous chapter, the UK economy has become increasingly dominated since the crisis by the services sector, with growth fastest in the service industries with lowest pay (Plunkett et al. 2014, pp. 31–34). The UK's post-crisis economy is a textbook example of what Anne Wren calls 'the services transition', characterised not only by transformation in the jobs we do, but also by how we do them, with services sector employment characterised by low pay and job volatility or casualisation, a reliance on human beings (rather than technology) that makes increasing productivity difficult, and a polarisation between low-skilled and high-skilled profession (so-called 'hollowing out') with little mobility between the two. Strong aggregate-level labour market performance in a services-led economy is invariably accompanied by an obfuscation of the traditional link between work and well-being (Wren 2013).

The Impotence of Active Labour Market Policy

The performance of the labour market in the UK since the financial crisis has far more to do with an intensification of the services transition than with the success of the coalition and Conservative governments' specific initiatives on employment policy. Although post-crisis economic policy in general has of course hastened structural change within the labour market, employment policy in particular has been little more than a bystander in terms direct policy impacts. This section argues, however, that the Conservative Party's limited changes to what is known in a UK context as 'active labour market policy' (ALMP) has played an important role in valorising work—just as welfare reform, as discussed in the next section, has played an important role in demonising worklessness.

ALMP is essentially a supply-side employment strategy; it encapsulates interventions designed to improve the employability of individuals, most specifically those seeking work—it can be contrasted with interventions designed to increase the *demand* for labour. Although supply-side interventions do not preclude demand-side interventions, in the UK, the emergence of the notion of an active labour market policy coincided with the partial (and now total) eschewal of Keynesian demand-side interventions in the late 1970s. There are three main forms of active labour market policy: firstly, support for individuals seeking work; the state will offer intermediary services so that job searches are more effective, or limited training in job acquisition skills. Secondly, support for individuals to improve or reorient their skills, to better match available job opportunities. Thirdly, the provision of employment subsidies; although subsidised employment might seem to suggest an anti-market orientation, in practice subsidies are generally designed either to improve the employability of jobseekers by enabling them to gain experience of work for a limited period, or encourage employers to offer existing job opportunities to people that have experienced unemployment. Despite rightly being considered a progenitor in the turn across Europe to a supply-side employment strategy, the UK spends very little on active labour market policy-based interventions, and what it does spend is heavily concentrated on the first form, that is, support for individuals in seeking employment opportunities. Unfortunately, the latest comparable data for ALMP expenditure by the UK government relates only to 2010. At that point, the UK spent around 0.4 per cent of GDP on ALMP measures, around three-quarters of which was on job acquisition services. Expenditure by Germany, France, and the European Union as a whole in this area was broadly equivalent, but they also spent, respectively, 0.5 per cent, 0.8 per cent, and 0.5 per cent of GDP on other forms of ALMP-based support, notably training and employment subsidies (in the case of Germany) and direct job creation (in the case of France).[5]

Although it is impossible to construct an exact figure, there is no reason to believe that the coalition government spent considerably more than this after 2010—and good reasons to conclude that it has spent considerably less. The coalition's flagship ALMP measure, the Work Programme, now costs slightly less than its predecessor (the Flexible New Deal (FND)), that is, approximately £600 million (or 0.04 per cent of GDP; it originally cost much less) (DWP 2012, 2014). The bulk of ALMP expenditure is via Jobcentre Plus (JCP) (which offers support before individuals enter the Work Programme) and, to a much lesser extent, local authorities—both of which have had their operational budgets cut significantly. Although more funds for ALMP were available in the pre-crisis period, and again in the immediate post-crisis period before 2010, coalition policy is largely a continuation of New Labour's welfare-to-work regime. The Blair government introduced the New Deal in 1998, aimed predominantly at young people. The New Deal for Young People offered persons aged under 25 who had been unemployed for six months intense job search support for four months, generally through JCP. If this programme failed to lead to employment, participants were offered one of four options: full-time education or training for a year, subsidised employment in the private sector for six months (with some support for on-the-job training), subsidised employment in the voluntary sector, or a six-month public sector work placement via the Environmental Task Force. Participants continued to receive Jobseekers' Allowance (JSA), the principal out-of-work benefit, during their time on the New Deal (or slightly higher payments if in subsidised private sector employment); participation in the New Deal was mandatory, if individuals wished to continue to receive JSA. A similar programme was available to people aged 25 or over that had been unemployed for 18 months, and there were tailored New Deal programmes for older workers, disabled people, and lone parents. Despite the availability of training and employment subsidies for the long-term unemployed, the vast majority of New Deal expenditure was focused on job acquisition services (Berry 2014e, p. 19).

In 2007, Labour effectively abandoned all of the elements of the New Deal that were not focused on job acquisition support, by introducing the FND. The innovation of FND was related not to the form of ALMP support it offered, but rather its delivery by private or voluntary sector providers, rather than simply JCP. Yet Gordon Brown quickly reintroduced the training and employment subsidy elements of the original New Deal in 2008, under the Train to Gain and Future Jobs Fund programmes, when the financial crisis led to a rise in unemployment (Berry 2014e, p. 23). Both were abolished in 2010. It is worth reiterating that, as under New Labour, the majority of job acquisition services continue to be delivered through the JCP, in the form of advisory services, given that most JSA recipients find work relatively quickly (work/welfare 'cycling' is a major issue within the UK labour market, as individuals find employment fairly straightforwardly, but are unable to sustain it [McCollum 2013]). Under the coalition's regime, after a year in receipt of JSA, or nine months for those aged 18–24, employment support for unemployed people is handed over to Work Programme providers. These providers are private companies commissioned centrally by the Department for Work and Pensions (DWP), paid on a 'payment-by-results' basis, although provision is now organised regionally rather than nationally. Crucially, the 'result' is not simply the obtainment of a job by a participant; full payment usually depends on employment being maintained for at least 18 months over a two-year period. However, it does not depend on a single position being sustained over this time—providers can obtain full payment by placing participants in several temporary jobs consecutively.

Paradoxically, despite the significant increase in employment, the Work Programme cannot be considered a success in any direct sense. In its first two years of operation, the Work Programme performed below expectations. The measure devised by the Centre for Economic and Social Inclusion (CESI) (2013), based on participants obtaining employment for a year, shows that the programme has performed consistently below a minimum performance level (i.e., an estimation of the 'dead-weight' level). Performance improved throughout 2012, but CESI argues that it plateaued in 2013. Data published by DWP in 2014 shows that only 48,000 full 'sustainment' payments had been made to Work Programme providers at that point—representing just over 3 per cent of cases referred to the Work Programme since June 2011 (Rawlinson 2014). The principal reason for the ostensible failure of the Work Programme is that employment growth has far exceeded policymakers' expectations, meaning that those entering the programme are predominantly individuals that face the highest hurdles to formal employment. JCP's sanctions regime, discussed below, has effectively disciplined any individual who is able to work in some form against any degree of circumspection regarding the job opportunities they pursue.

However, the notion that the Work Programme—or the Conservative Party's approach to ALMP more generally—has failed overlooks the ideological or discursive role being played by the policy in this regard. In short, the Work Programme has little direct impact on most people, even those that experience unemployment, but it serves to reinforce certain behavioural norms in relation to the labour market, most specifically the imperative for individuals to always be available for work of any description (Berry 2014c, pp. 605, 606). Addressing the welfare-to-work agenda in his 2010 party conference speech, David Cameron remarked that '[f] airness means giving people what they deserve—and what people deserve depends on how they behave. If you really cannot work, we'll look after you. But if you can work, but refuse to work, we will not let you live off the hard work of others' (Cameron 2010a). Although rather similar to the New Deal, and certainly the FND, in operation, it is revealing that the coalition government moved away from the language of a 'deal' between individuals and the state; under the Work Programme, individuals have no agency whatsoever, only the non-negotiable duty to seek employment. Moreover, the designation suggests—or confirms—that ALMP is the main means by which the state provides or facilitates work and, as such, serves to further delegitimise the notion that the state is able to create jobs. In this sense, the valorisation of work is the ideal and necessary accompaniment to creating self-sufficiency through austerity. We have witnessed, therefore, in the hands of Conservative politicians, a perversion of what 'full employment' means. It is no longer understood as something that governments might pursue, but rather something that governments might simply *expect* a highly liberalised labour market, and effectively disciplined workforce, to deliver. Championing full employment does not therefore represent a defence of the state's ability to bring full employment about, but rather a valorisation of a comprehensively privatised and individualised labour market as the antithesis of state intervention.

Austerity and Welfare

If the principal aim of austerity in normative terms is to establish self-sufficiency at the individual level, then scaling back social security entitlements is the logical corollary of the insistence that individuals find work by any means necessary. This is partly achieved by the Conservative Party in government quite crudely cutting a wide range of benefits, in a seemingly ad hoc manner. We can also point to the tightening of conditionality for jobseekers—where ALMP and social policy overlap—which enables only limited savings. However, it is also the case that some elements of social security have seen expenditure increase, insofar as increased spending serves the longer-term goal of redefining the nature of the welfare state and individuals' relationship with it. Overall, benefit expenditure has fallen *as a proportion of GDP* since 2010, yet was the same *in real terms* in 2015/2016 as it was in 2010/2011, that is, around £220 billion (this is explained by GDP rising faster than inflation) (Hood 2015; OBR 2014b). We should not doubt that the Conservative Party have sought, and will seek, to reduce benefit expenditure—creating hardship for many in the process. But it seems that the ideological assault on the idea of welfare seems to be just as important, if not more so, as actual savings.

One of the highest profile cuts has been the imposition of a 'cap' on the amount of benefits that households can receive, generally £26,000 per year (the cap differs for different types of households in different locations, and not all benefits are covered by the cap; not to be confused with the 'welfare cap', discussed in the next chapter). However, although affecting some families significantly, the benefits cap is a largely symbolic measure, saving less than £300 million per year (BBC News 2012). The main cap is expected to be lowered to £23,000 from 2016, but may be reduced to £20,000 outside London. There have been changes to eligibility and benefit calculation rules relating to Housing Benefit for private tenants, saving around £2 billion per year, but also the decision to cut what is referred to by the government as the 'spare room subsidy' for recipients in social housing—a measure known more commonly as the 'bedroom tax'. This results in Housing Benefit being partially withdrawn from people who have unused bedrooms in their home; it has been controversial on several fronts, most obviously a limited supply of smaller properties in some areas into which families may relocate—so they have no choice but to pay the tax. The measure saves far less than other changes to Housing Benefit, around £350 million per year, but is perhaps the only benefit cut which was strongly opposed by the Labour opposition before 2015. These changes are strongly outweighed by upward pressure on the Housing Benefit bill, which now exceeds £25 billion per year. Similarly, a range of cuts to disability benefits amounting to savings of around £1.7 billion per year have been offset by higher caseloads (Hood and Phillips 2015). The coalition government also announced a 10 per cent cut in funds for Council Tax Benefit, available to people in receipt of certain means-tested benefits—yet it at the same time localised the benefit, meaning that local authorities could decide how to implement the cut. The most significant benefit savings have come from capped increases rather than actual cuts, with most working-age benefits having a 1 per cent indexation cap imposed from 2013 onwards (in addition to permanent savings associated with switching to CPI indexation) and others being frozen altogether. These changes have saved around £6 billion per year, although actual savings have again been mitigated by higher caseloads for some of the benefits affected (Hood and Phillips 2015).

A further example of a significant welfare change that is not actually designed to reduce expenditure (beyond a negligible amount) is the coalition government's strengthening of conditionality in the receipt of JSA, as noted in the previous section. Conditionality has of course long existed in relation to out-of-work benefit receipt, but the coalition has significantly increased the use of sanctions (i.e., benefit withdrawal) for those failing to satisfy certain behavioural expectations. The government introduced Mandatory Work Activity (MWA), a scheme which primarily consists of four-week work placements of up to 30 hours per week (delivered by private contractors) for JSA recipients not yet eligible for the Work Programme. In the first year of MWA, 46 per cent of those referred to the programme by JCP either gave up JSA voluntarily as a result or had it removed when they failed to complete their placement (DWP 2013). In 2014, the coalition introduced the Help to Work (HTW) scheme—for benefit claimants that failed to find a job through the Work Programme. Through HTW, people who have been unemployed for around three years lose JSA unless they agree to a six-month 'community work placement', attend a JCP site every day to report on job seeking activity, or enter an intensive JCP engagement programme (HM Government 2014). The scheme was piloted in 2013, and an evaluation found that participants were only 2–4 per cent less likely to be claiming benefits at the end of the programme than non-participant JSA claimants (DWP 2014). While the sanctions regime remains in place, the work placement elements of JSA appear now to have been ended, with their ideological benefits deemed insufficient to justify their cost in the 2015 round of departmental spending cuts (Bates 2015). Interestingly, DWP was forced to apologise in 2015 after it emerged that the case studies of the positive impact of benefit sanctions it was using in its promotional literature around welfare to work were fake (Stone 2015). It is worth noting that the Conservative government remains in the process of implementing (after significant delays) Universal Credit (UC) to replace a range of benefits, principally JSA and the most important tax credits for those in work. UC was not necessarily conceived as a spending cut and, as originally envisaged (like the Work Programme, it was developed in opposition by former Conservative Party leader, and subsequently Work and Pensions Secretary [until March 2016], Iain Duncan Smith), would have cost slightly more than the systems it replaces, while ostensibly improving financial incentives to attain employment (Brewer et al. 2011)—although, as discussed below, it will end up being far less generous than originally intended.

The Conservative Party's most coherent policy on welfare expenditure is probably its protection of expenditure on pensioner benefits. The new 'single-tier' state pension is nominally fiscally neutral (although does represent a significant cut in entitlement for some groups), but expenditure on the state pension has in fact risen significantly due to the 'triple-lock' indexation policy of annually uprating pensions in payment by earnings, inflation, or 2.5 per cent. The most cynical rationale for this policy orientation points to the growing power of 'the grey vote'—with older people more likely to support the Conservative Party. A more sophisticated, and sympathetic, explanation would recognise that targeting pensioners for benefit cuts might help to achieve the goals of austerity as conventionally understood in terms of reducing public spending, but would contribute little to the broader aims of austerity in terms of reorienting attitudes and behaviours towards the labour market. Interestingly, the coalition government did make some savings on pensioner benefit expenditure, by quickening the pace of state pension age increases—thereby effectively widening the pool of people expected to provide for their own financial security through work. Such changes have been strongly opposed by groups representing older people. Furthermore, we have to recognise the subtle role being played by increased expenditure on the state pension in encouraging people to make greater use of the private pensions system to provide for their financial security in retirement. In combination with the introduction of a flat-rate state pension, it is envisaged that the state pension will in future provide a stable platform for private savings, rather than in itself representing a social insurance-style mechanism for deferring earnings over the life course. Of course, the reality is rather messier than this—but the ideological recasting of the state pension is the government's most important objective (Berry 2014a).

Tax credits, predominantly aimed at 'the working poor', were not immune from the coalition government's benefit cuts. They were of course affected by the benefits cap and most significantly the restrictions on indexation. Most importantly, changes to the thresholds at which tax credit income is withdrawn when earnings rise, and the introduction of a disregard when earnings drop, led to significantly lower tax credit awards for many people. Savings were partially offset by increasing the generosity of Child Tax Credit for many recipients (Hood and Phillips 2015). However, it was revealed after the 2015 general election that a significant portion of the promised welfare savings of £12 billion per year—a commitment made, with few accompanying details, in the Conservative Party's manifesto—would come from further cuts to tax credits, again via changes to income thresholds and taper rates. Modelling by the Resolution Foundation suggested that many families would lose more than £1000 per year as a result, with households with more than one child the worst affected, and two-thirds of the savings arising from cuts to benefits received by the poorest 30 per cent of households (Finch 2015). However, in a constitutionally dubious move, the House of Lords rejected the secondary legislation that would have enabled these changes to be made, forcing George Osborne to introduce the planned cuts more slowly, essentially by delaying them until UC has been implemented in place of existing tax credits. As such, UC *will* look like a cut when fully introduced and will act to make employment significantly less lucrative for many individuals. Of course, the Conservative government is eager for individuals to secure a decent income wholly from private employment, rather than relying on the state—and indeed expectant that austerity-related adjustments will enable such circumstances over the long term.

However, this does not mean that the government would necessarily have chosen to make these specific cuts were it not for the perceived electoral imperative to be seen as tough on welfare, given how successfully their own austerity narrative has penetrated the public consciousness. One of the implications of the move to reduce tax credit or future UC entitlements, amid the continuing sluggishness in earnings growth, is George Osborne's 2015 decision to rebrand the national minimum wage as the 'national living wage' and indeed promise a significant increase in its rate over the medium term. Osborne's skills as a political tactician in appropriating a cause traditionally associated with the left were lauded as a result, yet it seems unlikely that in more favourable circumstances, the Conservative Party would be comfortable endorsing the idea that the state has a role in ensuring that private sector wages are set according to actual living costs (even if, again, the policy reality is messier in practice). The purpose of austerity is to demonstrate that by accepting self-sufficiency and the logic of the market, and therefore less dependence on the collective mechanisms of the state (such as the setting of wage floors, especially ones nominally linked to the cost of living), we will all be better off in the long run.

Conclusion

George Osborne has claimed that increasing employment is 'a central goal of our economic plan' (cited in Watt and Mason 2014). This is hardly a novel statement for a Chancellor of the Exchequer to make, but what is novel is the message he is really trying to convey, that is, that increasingly employment is an important, if not the most important, *measure* of the success of the coalition and Conservative governments' economic policy agenda. Employment should of course be a measure of economic success, but the austerity agenda appears to elevate it above all others, therefore marginalising concerns that increasing employment at all costs might actually be contributing to erstwhile signs of labour market failure, such as stagnating productivity, pay, and living standards. It is important to place this sentiment in the context of the Conservative Party's apparent diagnosis of what caused the financial crisis, that is, excessive welfarism. As such, employment, as a measure, is defined more by what it *is not* than what it *is*. If you are in work, you are on the path to self-sufficiency rather than state dependence. The nature of that work is, for policymakers, a secondary consideration.

As noted in the third section, however, economic reality does not always conform to the ideal of self-sufficiency. For example, in order to justify an attack on welfare dependence for those that are already in work, the Conservative government has been compelled to endorse the idea that the state has a legitimate role in setting an ambitious wage floor related to the actual cost of living. This reminds us that while austerity is a proxy for legitimising individual self-sufficiency (occasionally an imperfect one), self-sufficiency is itself a proxy for legitimising the resurrection of the pre-crisis growth model. Intensifying the long standing move towards welfare retrenchment serves multiple purposes in this regard, most notably the creation of a large, flexible, compliant, and poorly rewarded workforce which suits the short-term tendencies of UK business, with private sector enterprises disinclined to invest in capital-intense production. It also creates, more indirectly, greater demand for financial services and exacerbates reliance on personal wealth as source of financial well-being—both of which have implications for the macroeconomic role of the finance sector and the housing market in the UK. Yet policy elites' strategy in this regard is not guaranteed to succeed; they are seeking to re-establish many of the core elements of a pre-crisis growth model, but eschewing others (such as large-scale public investment in depressed regions), and in less favourable circumstances (such as greater scrutiny over and controls on finance sector activities and uncertain international economic conditions). Such difficulties have necessitated the appropriation of hitherto left-wing causes such as full employment and the living wage, in ways that may leave the government's strategy vulnerable to attack from the left. As such, the ideological agenda replete in how welfare retrenchment is justified, insofar as it represents an attempt to establish a hegemonic influence over the norms that underpin economic life, is just as important as what policy looks like in practice.

Notes

1. Data on employment and unemployment across Europe and selected OECD countries were downloaded from the European Commission's Eurostats website, available at http://ec.europa.eu/eurostat/web/lfs/data/main-tables.
2. Data on average weekly earnings were downloaded from the Office for National Statistics' regular labour market bulletins, available at

http://ons.gov.uk/ons/rel/lms/labour-market-statistics/november-2015/statistical-bulletin.html.

3. Data on productivity were downloaded from the Office for National Statistics' regular labour productivity bulletins, available at http://ons.gov.uk/ons/rel/productivity/labour-productivity/q1–2015/stbq115.html.
4. Data on temporary employment, self-employment, and employment by age group were downloaded from the Office for National Statistics' regular labour market bulletins, available at http://ons.gov.uk/ons/rel/lms/labour-market-statistics/november-2015/statistical-bulletin.html.
5. Data on ALMP expenditure across Europe and selected OECD countries were downloaded from the European Commission's Eurostats website, available at http://ec.europa.eu/eurostat/web/labour-market/labour-market-policy/main-tables.

References

Bates, F. (2015). Why no fanfare to the end of workfare? *Touchstone*, November 27. http://touchstoneblog.org.uk/2015/11/why-no-fanfare-to-the-end-of-workfare/. Accessed 28 Nov 2015.

BBC News. (2012, 23 January). Government suffers Lords defeat over benefit cap plan. http://www.bbc.co.uk/news/uk-politics-16675314. Accessed 10 Nov 2015.

Berry, C. (2014a). Austerity, ageing and the financialisation of pensions policy in the UK. *British Politics,* November 10. http://dx.doi.org/10.1057/bp.2014.19

Berry, C. (2014c). Quantity over quality: A political economy of 'active labour market policy' in the UK. *Policy Studies*, *35*(6), 592–610.

Berry, C. (2014e). The hyper-Anglicisation of active labour market policy: Facilitating and exemplifying a flawed growth model. Sheffield Political Economy Research Institute paper no. 14. http://speri.dept.shef.ac.uk/wp-content/uploads/2014/08/SPERI-Paper-No.-14-The-hyper-Anglicisation-of-active-labour-market-policy.pdf. Accessed 9 Nov 2014.

Berry, C., & Hay, C. (2015). Has the UK economy been 'rebalanced'? Sheffield Political Economy Research Institute British Political Economy Brief no. 14. http://speri.dept.shef.ac.uk/wp-content/uploads/2015/07/Brief14-Has-the-UK-economy-been-rebalanced.pdf. Accessed 20 Oct 2015.

Brewer, M., Browne, J., & Jin, W. (2011). Universal credit: A preliminary analysis. Institute for Fiscal Studies Briefing Note no. 116. http://www.ifs.org.uk/publications/5415. Accessed 10 Nov 2015.

Cameron, D. (2010a). Party conference speech. Speech delivered on 6 October 2010. http://www.theguardian.com/politics/2010/oct/06/david-cameron-speech-tory-conference. Accessed 10 Nov 2015.

Centre for Economic and Social Inclusion. (2013). *Work programme statistics: Inclusion analysis*. http://stats.cesi.org.uk/website_documents/WP_stats_inclusion_briefing_September_2013.pdf. Accessed 1 Nov 2015.

Clark, T. (2015). *Hard times: Inequality, recession and aftermath*. London: Yale University Press.

Department for Work and Pensions. (2012). *Ad hoc analysis of flexible new deal costs*. https://www.gov.uk/government/uploads/system/uploads/attachment_data/file/223086/fnd_costs_1201.pdf. Accessed 10 Nov 2015.

Department for Work and Pensions. (2013). *Early impacts of mandatory work activity*. https://www.gov.uk/government/uploads/system/uploads/attachment_data/file/222938/early_impacts_mwa.pdf. Accessed 10 Nov 2015.

Department for Work and Pensions. (2014). *Work programme: Programme costs to 31 March 2014*. https://www.gov.uk/government/uploads/system/uploads/attachment_data/file/325995/Work_Programme_Costs_v7_2014-07-01.pdf. Accessed 10 Nov 2015.

Finch, D. (2015). *The tax credit crunch: How to limit the losses for low-income families*. Resolution Foundation. http://www.resolutionfoundation.org/wp-content/uploads/2015/11/Tax-credit-event-slides-Full.pdf. Accessed 10 Nov 2015.

HM Government. (2014). *Help to work: Nationwide drive to help the long-term unemployed into work*. https://www.gov.uk/government/news/help-to-work-nationwide-drive-to-help-the-long-term-unemployed-into-work. Accessed 10 Nov 2015.

Hood, A. (2015). *Options for reducing spending on social security*. Institute for Fiscal Studies. http://www.ifs.org.uk/uploads/gb/gb2015/Slides/9_Hood_benefits.pdf. Accessed 10 Nov 2015.

Hood, A., & Phillips, D. (2015). *Benefit spending and reforms: The coalition government's record*. Institute for Fiscal Studies. http://www.ifs.org.uk/uploads/publications/bns/BN160.pdf. Accessed 10 Nov 2015.

McCollum, D. (2013). Precarious transitions and labour market disadvantage: Using longitudinal data to explain the nature of work-welfare cycling. *Regional Studies, 47*(10), 1752–1765.

McKenzie, L. (2015). *Getting by: Estates, class and culture in austerity Britain*. Bristol: Policy.

O'Hara, M. (2015). *Austerity bites: A journey to the sharp end of cuts in the UK*. Bristol: Policy.

Office for Budget Responsibility. (2014b). *Welfare trends report: October 2014.* http://budgetresponsibility.org.uk/wordpress/docs/Welfare_trends_report_2014_dn2B.pdf. Accessed 10 Nov 2015.

Office for National Statistics. (2014a). *Self-employed workers in the UK: 2014.* http://www.ons.gov.uk/ons/dcp171776_374941.pdf. Accessed 10 Nov 2015.

Office for National Statistics. (2015b). *Contracts with no guaranteed hours: 2015 update.* http://www.ons.gov.uk/ons/publications/re-reference-tables.html?edition=tcm%3A77-413869. Accessed 10 Nov 2015.

Plunkett, J., Hurrell, A., & Whittaker, M. (2014). *The state of living standards.* Resolution Foundation. http://www.resolutionfoundation.org/publications/state-living-standards/. Accessed 4 Mar 2014.

Rawlinson, K. (2014). Work programme creates just 48,000 long-term jobs in three years. *The Guardian*, March 21. http://www.theguardian.com/society/2014/mar/21/work-programme-creates-48000-long-term-jobs-three-years. Accessed 10 Nov 2015.

Stone, J. (2015). DWP admits making up quotes by 'benefit claimants' saying sanctions helped them. *The Independent*, August 18. http://www.independent.co.uk/news/uk/politics/dwp-admits-making-up-quotes-by-benefit-claimants-saying-sanctions-helped-them-10460351.html. Accessed 10 Nov 2015.

Watt, M., & Mason, R. (2014). George Osborne makes commitment 'to fight for full employment' in Britain. *The Guardian*, March 31. http://www.theguardian.com/politics/2014/mar/31/george-osborne-full-employment-britain-inflation. Accessed 10 Nov 2015.

Wren, A. (Ed.). (2013). *The political economy of the services transition.* Oxford: Oxford University Press.

CHAPTER 5

Deficit Reduction and Budget Irresponsibility

Abstract The coalition and Conservative governments have repeatedly espoused that eliminating the budget deficit is their principal policy objective. Yet they have also repeatedly failed to meet their fiscal targets in this regard. Keynesian economists have criticised the intention to radically cut spending, but also identified an apparent relaxation of George Osborne's cuts agenda as decisive in the resumption of steady growth in 2013. However, a Keynesian analytical lens offers only a partial understanding of the relationship between austerity and fiscal policy. In practice, deficit reduction, even if never achieved, functions as a legitimising mechanism for the wider objectives of austerity—and this function has now been institutionalised in the form of the Office for Budget Responsibility.

Keywords Deficit reduction • Spending cuts • Borrowing • Austerity • Keynesianism • Office for Budget Responsibility

Since the financial crisis, the Conservative Party has consistently sought to improve its image with reference to things that it will not do, or perhaps more precisely, will not *cut*. Its most important pledge in this regard is to protect the National Health Service (NHS) budget in real terms. The

C. Berry, *Austerity Politics and UK Economic Policy*, Building a Sustainable Political Economy: SPERI Research & Policy, DOI 10.1057/978-1-137-59010-7_5

same protection has been applied to spending on primary and secondary schools (the largest part of the education budget), and the international aid budget has been maintained at 0.7 per cent of GDP, as recommended by the United Nations, since 2013 (a commitment now enshrined in statute). Promises to protect certain budgets, most notably aspects of policing and defence expenditure, have also been made in relation to particular spending decisions. In short, David Cameron and George Osborne have sought popularity in defending the state against themselves, that is, their own desire to radically reduce public spending. The reason that protecting certain budgets has largely replaced the possibility of *increasing* them in the policymakers armoury is that reducing, and ultimately eliminating, the budget deficit (the gap between what comes in to the Exchequer as revenue and what goes out as public spending) has been the overriding objective of the coalition and Conservative governments. A commitment to deficit reduction—even if progress towards the goal is uncertain—is the foundation of the Conservative Party's credibility as a party of government.

As such, its 2010 election manifesto repeatedly referred to the UK's 'debt crisis'. Its first two sentences read: 'Britain needs change: few can doubt this. Our national finances are mired in debt'. It continued: 'with the national debt already doubled, and at risk of doubling again, it is this debt… that threatens to kill the recovery' (Conservative Party 2010, pp. *vii*, 3). There were, of course, plenty of references, which seem almost comical in hindsight, to reducing private indebtedness and rebalancing the economy more generally (as discussed in the second and third chapters of this book), but reducing the deficit was the clear priority. In the coalition agreement signed by the Conservatives and the Liberal Democrats in 2010, after agreed priorities across 31 areas of policy were outlined, an unnumbered endnote explained that 'the deficit reduction programme takes precedence over any of the other measures in this agreement, and the speed of implementation of any measures that have a cost to the public finances will depend on decisions to be made in the Comprehensive Spending Review' (HM Government, 2010, p. 35). The Conservative Party's 2015 election manifesto lacked the emotive vernacular of its predecessor, but maintained that 'finishing the job' by 'eliminating the deficit entirely' would be a Conservative government's main priority. Indeed, despite Osborne's failure to meet his deficit reduction targets, the 2015 manifesto contained a fairly detailed justification of why it was now necessary for the deficit reduction agenda to become even more ambitious than what the coalition had attempted (Conservative Party 2015, pp. 8, 9). This mutual dependence of the necessity of cuts and the apparent progressiveness of selectively not cutting was typified by the Conservative Party's campaign posters in advance of the 2010 election. The most well-known example is notorious mainly because it featured a quite crudely 'airbrushed' image of David Cameron. Yet its text, attributed to Cameron, is more revealing for our purposes: '[w]e can't go on like this. Cut the deficit, not the NHS.' Not cutting the NHS budget of course increases the difficulty (at least in the short term) of cutting the deficit more generally—yet the intended message is that only a Conservative government, with its responsible approach to public spending, would be in a position to safeguard health spending.

Like all good fairy tales, there must be a villain, whose narratological purpose is to be vanquished by the hero. In the case of the UK's post-crisis political discourse, our villain is played by the pre-crisis Labour Party (the instincts of which, so the story goes, remain evident in the post-crisis Labour Party too). As discussed in the introductory chapter, this view of the Blair and Brown governments is extraordinarily inaccurate. This is not the place to evaluate Labour's economic stewardship in general, but it is clear that the relatively high level of public investment before 2008 was not the cause of the significant budget deficit and borrowing levels that ensued after the financial crisis. Gordon Brown's commitment to 'prudence' marked him out as a fiscally conservative Chancellor. His 'golden rule' decreed that, over the economic cycle, borrowing was only permitted to increase to fund investment (rather than current spending), and the 'sustainable investment rule' decreed that, over the economic cycle, net public sector debt would be held below 40 per cent of GDP. Up to 2007, Brown may have 'fiddled the books a bit' in order to demonstrate that these rules had been adhered to (by altering the definition of the economic cycle and holding fiscal liabilities related to the Private Finance Initiative 'off the books'), but in general New Labour was far from profligate in its management of the public finances (Skidelsky 2015a). After the financial crisis, Brown, then prime minister, embraced deficit reduction by passing the Fiscal Responsibility Act 2010, which committed the government to halve borrowing by 2013/14, an objective to be achieved by fiscal consolidation of around 6 per cent of GDP between 2010 and 2014 (Lee 2015, p. 19). Nevertheless, the Conservatives' 2010 manifesto was littered with references to Labour's profligacy in office. The document asked the electorate for their 'consent for a programme of public spending control that will deal with Labour's debt crisis', and explained that the Office for Budget Responsibility (OBR) would 'ensure that no Labour government can ever attempt to bankrupt our public finances again' (Conservative Party 2010, pp. *ix*, 8). In introducing the notion of 'the big society', the manifesto argued that 'despite Labour's massive expansion of the state, many people's quality of life is getting worse, not better'.

The Labour bogey remained a constant feature of the Conservative Party's discourse once in office. For example, in 2014, David Cameron described Labour leader Ed Miliband and shadow chancellor Ed Balls as 'people who seem to have learned absolutely nothing from what went wrong with our economy, that the problems were based on too much borrowing, too much spending, too much debt' (cited in Mason 2014). The notion that the Conservatives represented 'competence', in contrast to the 'chaos' that would result from overspending by a Miliband government, was a constant refrain of the Conservatives' pre-2015 election rhetoric (see Conservative Party 2015). We can of course question the extent to which the Conservative Party has, in government, genuinely prioritised deficit reduction, given the selective nature of spending cuts and its willingness to introduce or exacerbate various fiscal risks. This book has already discussed at various points the inconsistencies in how austerity, as conventionally understood, has been implemented in practice in this regard. This chapter further explores the meaning and implications of the specific commitment to deficit reduction. The first section details the nature of the promises made, and revised, by George Osborne and discusses the value and limitations of the Keynesian critique of the deficit reduction agenda. The second section shows how the apparent necessity of the deficit reduction agenda helped the coalition government to effectively decontest the key tenets of austerity, in the form of the OBR.

Austerity and Economics

It would appear that very few leading macroeconomists support deficit reduction; at the very least, those who do rarely articulate this view in public. It is generally acknowledged that the early post-crisis consensus throughout North America and Europe in favour of deficit reduction was influenced by research by American economists Carmen Reinhart and Kenneth Rogoff, and Italian economists Alberto Alesina and Silvia Ardagna, which has subsequently been widely disputed. Both Reinhart and Rogoff (2010) and Alesina and Ardagna (2009) produced research that, essentially, demonstrated that public debt impedes economic growth, yet as Paul Krugman explains:

> All of the economic research that allegedly supported the austerity push has been discredited. Widely touted statistical results were, it turned out, based on highly dubious assumptions and procedures—plus a few outright mistakes—and evaporated under closer scrutiny. It is rare, in the history of economic thought, for debates to get resolved this decisively. The austerian discourse that dominated elite discourse five years ago has collapsed, to the point where hardly anyone still believes it. (Krugman 2015)

What Krugman essentially represents, of course, alongside well-known macroeconomists in the UK making similar arguments—such as academics Simon Wren-Lewis (2015) and Robert Skidelsky (2015a), *Financial Times* columnist Martin Wolf (2013), former Cabinet Office chief economist Jonathan Portes (2013), and former Monetary Policy Committee (MPC) member David Blanchflower (2015)—is a mainstream revival of Keynesian thought. The Keynesians eventually came to influence the International Monetary Fund (IMF) (or at least its chief economist Olivier Blanchard, who left the organisation in October 2015), which admitted that its belief in favour of 'expansionary fiscal contraction' in 2010 had been based on faulty analysis and unduly influenced by its experience of addressing problems in the Eurozone periphery (Wren-Lewis 2015). It is fair to conclude that the Keynesians have, in purely intellectual terms, and aided by the sluggish recoveries in countries with the most austere fiscal regimes, fairly comprehensively won the argument that governments should increase expenditure during a downturn, irrespective of budget deficits, and that spending cuts will suppress demand and prolong negative or weak growth.

According to Krugman (2015), 'the doctrine that ruled the world in 2010 has more or less vanished from the scene. Except in Britain'. He describes the UK as 'stuck on obsessions that have been mainly laughed out of the discourse elsewhere'. Krugman's (2010) view that the pro-austerity argument rests ultimately upon 'the confidence fairy' helps to explain the resonance of deficit reduction in the UK. According to Skidelsky, the idea that private economic actors will be reluctant to invest if public spending is too high (fearing future tax rises and a 'crowding out' of market activity) has been a persistent feature of UK economic statecraft, forming a central element of 'the Treasury view'; indeed, this idea fuelled resistance to the adoption of a Keynesian response to the Great Depression (Skidelsky 2015b, pp. 4, 5). The fact that the coalition government palpably failed to reduce the deficit along its desired timetable, having suppressed the early signs of recovery in 2010 and presided over economic stagnation in 2011 and 2012, serves as vindication of the Keynesian view. In 2010, Osborne had promised to eliminate the structural budget deficit by 2014/15, with net borrowing falling from around 10 per cent to around 2 per cent of GDP over this period, and net debt beginning to fall from a height of 70 per cent of GDP. In 2012, the deficit reduction timetable was extended by two years to 2016/17, with an acknowledgement that net debt would rise to almost 80 per cent of GDP. In 2013, the timetable was extended by a further two years to 2018/19; it was around this time that the Conservatives began to refer to the 'long-term economic plan', described by Simon Lee as 'a simple rhetorical recognition of the obvious truth that the coalition would fail to achieve its planned fiscal consolidation within the timetable specified in June 2010' (Lee 2015, pp. 23, 24). In late 2014, however, the ambition of the plan was actually increased, with Osborne promising a budget surplus of 1 per cent of GDP by 2019/20 (thus eliminating the current, as well as structural, budget deficit). This preceded the proposal in 2015 for a statutory Charter for Budget Responsibility, which would commit the government to running a surplus in most economic circumstances. The charter was, of course, a political ploy. After the 2015 election, it provided the ideal trap for Labour's new leadership; Labour's left-wing shadow chancellor, John McDonnell, originally promised to support the charter, assuming that it offered an opportunity to articulate a Keynesian-inspired, growth-led deficit reduction agenda. The right of the Labour Party (heavily defeated in the leadership election, but nevertheless well-represented in the parliamentary party) welcomed the decision, only for McDonnell to change his mind once he became more familiar with the specific policy implications of the charter. It should be noted that after the election the timetable for reaching the 1 per cent surplus was delayed by Osborne, by a year, to 2020/21—although the OBR forecast that the chances of this being achieved were only 50/50 (Syal 2015). Interestingly, Liam Stanley (2015a) argues that the repeated postponement of the deficit reduction end date may actually mean that austerity is succeeding, because austerity is fundamentally a future-oriented narrative where the journey towards a debt- or deficit-free future is more important than the actual destination. It is also worth noting that a self-imposed cap on welfare expenditure (announced in early 2014), which would have restricted overall spending on most benefits from 2016/17, is now expected to be breached in the first three years.

One of the limitations of the Keynesian critique of austerity, however, is that deficit reduction—and specifically reducing borrowing—has not actually been a particularly important agenda for the coalition or Conservative governments. As such, the response of many macroeconomists has consisted of both criticising the spending cuts agenda, while demonstrating that Osborne has surreptitiously abandoned the agenda, after the stagnation of 2010 and 2011 (see Portes 2013). For this reason, so the argument goes, steady GDP growth finally resumed in 2013, with higher spending is some areas continuing in 2014 (Tilly 2015; see Murphy and Palan [2015] for discussion of what types of government spending have, and have not, been cut). Does this vindicate the Keynesian view? The obvious conclusion may be that the Keynesians were right: early efforts by the coalition to reduce the deficit destroyed the recovery already underway by the time of the 2010 election, but the moderation of Osborne's plan from around 2012 onwards has demonstrated the value of public spending after a downturn. However, while the Keynesian perspective appears to help us to understand the *economics* of narrow deficit reduction objectives, it is less able to help us understand the *political economy* of the broader austerity agenda. Indeed, the Keynesian perspective grew to renewed prominence in public debates immediately before and after the 2015 election (replicating debates from the 2010 election), as the Conservative Party sought to defend their plans for the fiscal charter and budget surplus. The Keynesians should have known that the policy reality would again fail to match the rhetoric. Accordingly, when in November 2015 changes to the OBR's modelling led to significantly improved fiscal forecasts for the 2015–2020 parliament, Osborne chose not to maintain the pace of deficit reduction, so as to reduce borrowing over a shorter period, but rather to again stagger the application of welfare and departmental spending cuts. The Keynesians were thus left fighting a phantom menace, at least partially of their own making due to a tendency to see the politics of austerity in terms of a binary choice between higher and lower public spending.

The lesson is clearly that deficit reduction cannot be taken at face value. A slower pace of deficit reduction may have been pursued, but nevertheless there have been some severe cuts in public spending, and many expected cuts in welfare spending have been thwarted by economic problems discussed throughout this book. The sluggish growth the UK economy has experienced is not simply a product of decisions around public expenditure; the international environment is a conditioning factor, and we also need to consider how the particular approach to deficit reduction that has been pursued corresponds to the wider model of economic growth. For example, in Keynesian theory, a textbook approach deficit reduction would encompass tax rises to increase government revenue. Yet coalition and Conservative fiscal policy has been characterised by fairly significant tax cuts, primarily to income tax for middle-income households (as the tax-free personal allowance has risen significantly) and corporation tax (the main rate of which will have fallen from 28 to 18 per cent by 2020—lower than any other G20 country), and stamp duty on property purchases. Taxation policies may not correspond perfectly with a Keynesian perspective (the most obvious discrepancy would be the coalition government's decision to raise value added tax (VAT) from 17.5 to 20 per cent in 2011), yet the implication overall is that the Conservative Party has been content to forgo additional revenues, which would have helped to reduce the deficit, in order to reduce the tax burden on employment, profits, and the housing market. The deficit reduction timetable announced before the 2015 election stipulates that 98 per cent of the required fiscal consolidation would be achieved by spending cuts, with tax rises contributing only 2 per cent (Lee 2015, p. 25). In both the 2010 and 2015 manifestos, criticism of the higher spending or borrowing and higher taxes that would apparently be a result of electing a Labour government invariably go together in the same breath; indeed, the 2010 manifesto has as many references to 'Labour's jobs tax' (a small rise in National Insurance contributions) as it does to 'Labour's debt crisis'. It seems unlikely that the 98/2 balance between spending cuts and tax rises will actually be upheld (in the previous five years, the balance between spending cuts and tax rises had been 82/18), but if there are tax rises, they will be implemented early in the life of the Conservative majority government, and in areas less visible to the electorate. Accordingly, in November 2015, Osborne introduced an 'apprenticeship levy' on many private companies—an attempt to offset corporation tax cuts presented disingenuously as investment in occupational training. He also increased stamp duty on buy-to-let property purchases (which had been recommended by the Bank of England) and enabled local authorities to raise council tax rates to compensate for ongoing cuts in central government funding for local services.

Wolfgang Streeck's (2014) analysis of 'the debt state' is arguably more helpful to us than a Keynesian framework in seeking to understand the coalition and Conservative governments' pursuit of deficit reduction. For Streeck, the European 'tax state' has evolved into a debt state, in which wealthy individuals and enterprises are no longer as prepared to fund government activity through taxation, and as such, public borrowing increases. As such, argues Streeck, public debt has become pivotal to 'buying time', that is, maintaining a neoliberal economic order as contemporary capitalism struggled under the weight of its own contradictions, chiefly accelerating inequality and underinvestment. Accepting the relevance of this perspective for the UK requires us to dismiss a little too quickly the Conservative Party's anti-debt narrative as purely rhetorical, or even deceitful. While spending cuts have been more limited than we might have expected, we should not doubt the sincerity of Conservatives' efforts to retrench certain aspects of government activity over the long term, principally welfare entitlements. However, there has certainly been a shift of emphasis in Conservative rhetoric, towards the creation of a budget surplus, rather than reducing public debt. And the monetary policy response to the 2008 crisis (discussed in the second chapter)—supported and indeed continued by the Conservatives in government—demonstrates the centrality of public debt to sustaining the pre-crisis growth model, including its unorthodox use. As Streeck points out, 'the distinction between public and private money has become increasingly irrelevant... it is virtually impossible to tell where the state ends and the market begins, and whether governments have been nationalising the banks, or banks have been privatising the state' (2014, p. 40). Moreover, we can speculate that the demonisation of public debt by policy elites is in fact constitutive of attempts to increase its efficacy, insofar as bondholders are reassured by the state's apparent appetite to ensure its long-term solvency. This would help to explain the focus on retrenching citizens' entitlements rather than reducing actual spending in the short term, and indeed the attempt to undermine the ideological basis of increasing public expenditure even if actual levels of spending are not fully controllable at present. Accordingly, Kate Alexander Shaw (2015) argues that while the welfare cap, for instance, may technically be breached in the short term, its existence helps to shape discourse around the fiscal responsibilities of economic policymakers; additionally, the success of the austerity narrative in terms of proselytising behavioural change means that the Conservative Party can actually blame welfare recipients themselves, rather than their own economic stewardship, for breaches occurring.

Institutionalising Austerity

There is a growing body of work within political economy on the general public's view of austerity (Stanley 2015b, 2016); this is clearly an important factor in determining the extent to which the Conservative Party's agenda, pursued in tandem with the wider policy elite, will fare over the long term in relation to the goal of resurrecting and modifying the pre-crisis growth model. However, for political ideologies, the way in which their assumptions are institutionalised within the machinery of governance is as important as their ability to mobilise supporters (or inspire acquiescence). As such, the establishment of the OBR as the *de jure* guardian of the public finances is a vital aspect of post-crisis statecraft and austerity politics more generally, albeit one which has not yet received a great deal of scholarly attention. Nominally, the OBR provides independent fiscal and economic forecasts, through which the implications of government policy decisions for the economy and public finances can be credibly assessed. The mainstream media has largely accepted this understanding of the OBR's functions at face value (notwithstanding concerns about the extent of its independence, as discussed below), with then BBC economics editor Stephanie Flanders (2010), now of JP Morgan, reporting in 2010 that '[t] his government is going to be on a much shorter leash than the one that came before'. This section argues that the perception that the OBR acts as a constraint upon elected governments' fiscal policy manoeuvrability is far too simplistic. Insofar as George Osborne was on a shorter leash, it was one he placed willingly around his own neck.

Of course, as noted above, the Blair and Brown governments had designed their own fiscal leash, with the establishment of rules around borrowing in 1997. These rules may have been fairly malleable in practice, but at least provided a clear means by which Labour could be held to account, on its own terms, for its fiscal performance. The presentation of the OBR as a radical departure from Labour's approach is therefore inaccurate, but it is tempting to see the creation of OBR as a more substantive form of depoliticisation than Labour's rules-based approach, given the move away from self-regulation, and towards fiscal oversight by an independent body (cf. Flinders and Buller 2006; Wood and Flinders 2014). However, this would be a highly misleading conclusion to draw: if there is any continuity between Labour's fiscal rules and the work of the OBR, it is in that the latter's creation actually *increases* the fiscal flexibility afforded to the Chancellor. The OBR represents the abandonment of rules-based fiscal policy; it has no authority to prevent the government pursuing fiscal policy in whatever form it likes, only to forecast the implications. The agenda around resurrecting the pre-crisis growth model clearly demanded much greater flexibility for the coalition and Conservative governments to increase borrowing and maintain it at a relatively high level for a significant period of time. At the same time, however, the OBR plays an important—and perhaps unwitting—role in circumscribing the possibility of an elected government pursuing a more interventionist economic policy agenda, given that the fiscal implications would be immediately identified by the OBR.

The OBR was actually established by the Conservative Party *in opposition* in 2009—an effort by then shadow chancellor George Osborne to highlight the flaws in the Treasury's approach to forecasting under the Labour government. Osborne said that the OBR would 'hold a Conservative government to account for the promises it makes to the British people' (cited in BBC News 2009)—he was seizing upon Chancellor Alistair Darling's significant underestimate in 2008 of the extent to which the recession would increase borrowing, yet this was a mistake also committed by most other UK forecasters. Its first head was academic economist Sir Alan Budd, who had also led the shadow OBR. Given his support for the Conservative Party in opposition, Budd was unquestionably a political appointee, leading to early concerns about the OBR's independence from Osborne, some of which have now been addressed. Unlike the Treasury civil servants previously responsible for fiscal and economic forecasts, the Chancellor is solely responsible for appointing the head of the OBR and its executive board—Osborne has relinquished operational control of forecasting, but vastly increased his power of appointment in this area. Importantly, the Chancellor has also retained power over the *timing* of the publication of forecasts. It is also worth noting that the OBR, with only 19 full-time members of staff (including administrative support) (OBR 2015a), is firmly enmeshed in the Whitehall machinery and heavily reliant upon the Treasury, the Department for Work and Pensions (DWP), and HM Revenue and Customs for source information, as outlined in a Memorandum of Understanding between the departments (OBR 2011b). However, views on the authenticity of the OBR's independence quickly shifted in the government's favour when Budd unexpectedly resigned in 2010, to be replaced by the director of the Institute for Fiscal Studies (IFS), Robert Chote. The coalition government actually allowed Parliament (via the Treasury Select Committee) to approve Chote's appointment (a provision concretised in legislation in 2011, and extended to other executive members of the OBR's governing committee). Despite his marriage to Sharon White, a very senior Treasury official (now head of media regulator Ofcom), Chote was widely perceived as a more credibly independent voice at the top of the OBR.

There are, nevertheless, several examples of OBR decisions appearing to support the government's fiscal policy agenda. In the early years of the coalition, the OBR was frequently over-optimistic on overall economic growth, due largely to flaws in its modelling of business investment and productivity gains (Berry and Hay 2014, pp. 15, 16; Berry and Kirkland 2014, p. 4), and its assumption (which differed from best practice internationally) that each £1 cut in public expenditure took substantially less than £1 out of the economy (Murphy and Palan 2015, pp. 20–23). While such errors eventually become evident, when revised away in subsequent forecasts, other OBR decisions have had more lasting consequences. In December 2012, the OBR interpreted evidence of an upturn in GDP growth as evidence not of a purely cyclical upturn, but rather that the economy had not been as weakened by the recession as originally feared—therefore revising up 'the output gap' and revising down the structural deficit that Osborne was ostensibly seeking to eliminate (OBR 2012, pp. 33–46). Although other forecasters formed a similar view, Ian Mulheirn (2012), former senior Treasury official and director of the Social Market Foundation, remarked that the OBR had 'controversially moved the goalposts a big step closer to George Osborne's ball'. Similarly, as noted above, in November 2015, seemingly technical changes in the way that the OBR forecasts tax revenues and debt interest payments enabled Osborne to significantly dilute the severity of planned cuts to departmental budgets and welfare. At the same time, however, the OBR has occasionally embarrassed Osborne in its forecasting outputs, with Chote in particular appearing to relish such opportunities. In late 2014, the OBR reported that current spending would fall to levels not seen since the 1930s under the Chancellor's pre-election deficit reduction plans (OBR 2014a).

Yet this serves to underline the limitations of interpreting the significance of the OBR only through the lens of depoliticisation, that is, the extent of its independence from elected politicians. It is probably broadly correct to conclude that the willingness of Chote (and of course the statutory responsibility of the OBR to Parliament) to honestly and very publicly appraise progress along the coalition and Conservative governments' deficit reduction schedule has compelled Osborne to frequently postpone the point at which a balanced budget will be achieved. However, to conclude that this significant hampers the austerity agenda assumes that Osborne is highly motivated by deficit reduction—this appears not to be the case. Similarly, while the OBR eventually reported that deficit reduction would not be achieved along the coalition's original timetable, it could not report in real time on the shift in fiscal policy that at least partly explained this failure. As such, the existence of the OBR may help to create a sense of fiscal policy openness, but in reality Osborne has succeeded in remaining fairly reticent about his actual decision-making. Furthermore, while the OBR's statutory functions may necessitate a greater degree of honesty about the failure to date of deficit reduction, it does not assess the underlying economic problems that have led to the government failing to cut spending, or increase revenues, as quickly as it might have liked. This becomes especially problematic; however, if simply by existing, the OBR creates the sense that fiscal policy decisions are being 'supervised' by apolitical experts, thereby helping to shield the government from wider scrutiny. It should be noted that by legislating for the Charter for Budget Responsibility, and introducing measures such as the welfare cap, Osborne has imposed rule-based constraints on his fiscal policy approach reminiscent of those employed by New Labour, even if they differ markedly in content. Yet the existence of the OBR in an apparently supervisory role appears to be deflecting some of the critical attention away from Osborne in terms of whether such rules are adhered to.

Above all, what the existence of the OBR implies is that reducing the deficit matters—so much so that there is now a government agency devoted to it. With probity in the public finances elevated to a first-order political issue, it is not difficult to appreciate why public discourse appears to have assimilated seamlessly the notion that elected governments inherently misappropriate 'taxpayers' money'. Greater independence for the OBR may occasionally lead to embarrassment for Osborne, but also reinforces such trends, ultimately benefiting the Conservative agenda and how policy elites more generally have sought to respond to growth model failure. Indeed, former Cabinet Secretary Gus O'Donnell (commonly referred to as 'GOD' because of the range of his influence within the UK civil service in the 2000s) advocated in 2013 the creation of an Office of Taxpayer Responsibility to sit alongside the OBR. The new body would appraise the worth of all large items of public expenditure *before* they are implemented (effectively exercising a veto over spending decisions by directly elected governments), similar to the way that the National Audit Office appraises many policies with fiscal implications *after* they have been implemented

(O'Donnell 2013, pp. 384, 385; see also Berry and Berry 2014). It is highly unlikely that any government would agree to create such a body, as O'Donnell well knows—but that it has been advocated by such a prominent figure within the UK policy elite demonstrates the strength of the logic of depoliticised fiscal supervision in a discursive environment shaped by the austerity narrative.

Conclusion

Despite some academic research which preaches the case for deficit reduction and the reduction of public debt during an economic downturn (now largely discredited), it is clear that the case for austerity does not rest in macroeconomic theory. To a large extent, the debate about deficit reduction has been framed by its Keynesian opponents. Yet deficit reduction and austerity cannot be considered synonymous; a convincing intellectual challenge to the former has done little to dismantle the hegemony of the latter. Paradoxically, however, once we acknowledge that deficit reduction is, in part, an ideological fig leaf, we can begin to see more clearly that its valorisation and ultimately institutionalisation—even if it is not achieved in the foreseeable future—helps to both legitimate and shield from view the underlying objectives of the austerity agenda.

The 'folklore' often invoked by Conservative politicians (and occasionally others among the UK policy elite)—most frequently, the equation of the public finances with a household budget—explicitly invoke the politics of public debt and deficit reduction. Yet it also serves more subtly to support some of the assumptions that sustained the pre-crisis growth model, such as the limitations of an interventionist economic policy agenda, the inviolability of private property rights, and the primacy of private economic actors in the creation of wealth. The Conservative Party has been determined to demonise public debt in the post-crisis environment, but this narrative helps to obscure the fact that the UK growth model appears to have become highly dependent on public debt and, intriguingly, to reassure those that purchase public debt that their investments are secure.

References

Alesina, A., & Ardagna, S. (2009). *Large changes in fiscal policy: Taxes versus spending*. National Bureau of Economic Research working paper 15438. http://www.nber.org/papers/w15438. Accessed 10 Dec 2015.

BBC News. (2009, 8 December). Conservatives launch office for budget responsibility. http://news.bbc.co.uk/1/hi/uk_politics/8401517.stm. Accessed 29 Dec 2015.

Berry, C., & Berry, R. (2014). Better the devil: A response to Gus O'Donnell's 'better government'. *The Political Quarterly, 85*(1), 11–16.

Berry, C., & Hay, C. (2014). The great British 'rebalancing' act: The construction and implementation of an economic imperative for exceptional times. *British Journal of Politics and International Relations*, published online 12 December 2014. http://dx.doi.org/10.1111/1467-856X.12063

Berry, C., & Kirkland, C. (2014). Income tax revenue and economic change in the UK. Sheffield Political Economy Research Institute British Political Economy Briefno.9.http://speri.dept.shef.ac.uk/wp-content/uploads/2014/12/Brief9-Income-tax-revenue-and-economic-change-in-the-UK.pdf. Accessed 29 Dec 2015.

Blanchflower, D. (2015). George Osborne is set to make his sad state of affairs much worse with his lunatic plan. *The Independent*, June 14. http://www.independent.co.uk/news/business/comment/david-blanchflower/david-blanchflower-george-osborne-is-set-to-make-a-sad-state-of-affairs-much-worse-with-his-lunatic-10319605.html. Accessed 10 Dec 2015.

Flanders, S. (2010). "Why the Office for Budget Responsibility matters", *BBC News*, 17 May. http://www.bbc.co.uk/blogs/thereporters/stephanieflanders/2010/05/why_the_obr_matters.html. Accessed 10 Nov 2015.

Flinders, M., & Buller, J. (2006). Depoliticisation: Principles, tactics and tools. *British Politics, 1*(2), 293–318.

HM Government. (2010). *The coalition: Our programme for government*. https://www.gov.uk/government/uploads/system/uploads/attachment_data/file/78977/coalition_programme_for_government.pdf. Accessed 9 Nov 2015.

Krugman, P. (2010). The myths of austerity. *The New York Times*, 1 July. http://www.nytimes.com/2010/07/02/opinion/02krugman.html. Accessed 10 Dec 2015.

Krugman, P. (2015a). The myths of austerity. *The New York Times*, July 1. http://www.nytimes.co m/2010/07/02/opinion/02krugman.html. Accessed 10 Dec 2015.

Krugman, P. (2015b). The austerity delusion. *The Guardian*, April 29. http://www.theguardian.com/business/ng-interactive/2015/apr/29/the-austerity-delusion. Accessed 10 Dec 2015.

Lee, S. (2015). Indebted and unbalanced: The political economy of the coalition. In M. Beech & S. Lee (Eds.), *The Conservative-Liberal coalition: Examining the Cameron-Clegg government* (pp. 16–35). Basingstoke: Palgrave Macmillan.

Mason, R. (2014). David Cameron claims Ed Balls has 'learned noting' on public spending. *The Guardian*, January 27. http://www.theguardian.com/politics/2014/jan/27/david-cameron-ed-balls-public-spending-50p-tax. Accessed 10 Dec 2015.

Mulheirn, I. (2012). The OBR has opened a can of worms. *Social Market Foundation Blog*, December 7. http://www.smf.co.uk/the-obr-has-opened-a-can-of-worms/. Accessed 29 Dec 2015.

Murphy, R., & Palan, R. (2015). Why the UK's fiscal charter is doomed to fail: An analysis of austerity economics during the first and second Cameron governments. City Political Economy Research Centre working paper 2015/03. https://www.city.ac.uk/__data/assets/pdf_file/0003/296301/CITYPERC-WPS-201503.pdf. Accessed 29 Dec 2015.

O'Donnell, G. (2013). Better government. *The Political Quarterly, 84*(3), 380–387.

Office for Budget Responsibility. (2011b). *Memorandum of understanding between the office for budget responsibility, HM Treasury, Department for Work and Pensions and HM Revenue and Customs.* http://budgetresponsibility.org.uk/wordpress/docs/obr_memorandum040411.pdf. Accessed 29 Dec 2015.

Office for Budget Responsibility. (2012). *Economic and fiscal outlook: December 2012.* http://budgetresponsibility.org.uk/wordpress/docs/December-2012-Economic-and-fiscal-outlook23423423.pdf. Accessed 29 Dec 2015.

Office for Budget Responsibility. (2014a). *Economic and fiscal outlook: December 2014.* http://cdn.budgetresponsibility.independent.gov.uk/December_2014_EFO-web513.pdf. Accessed 29 Dec 2015.

Office for Budget Responsibility. (2015a). *Corporate and business plan: 2015/16 to 2017/18.* http://budgetresponsibility.org.uk/wordpress/docs/OBR-2015-16-to-2017-18-Business-plan.pdf. Accessed 29 Dec 2015.

Portes, J. (2013). What Osborne won't admit: Growth has increased because of slower cuts. *The New Statesman*, September 10. http://www.newstatesman.com/politics/2013/09/what-osborne-wont-admit-growth-has-increased-because-slower-cuts. Accessed 10 Dec 2015.

Reinhart, C. M., & Rogoff, K. S. (2010). Growth in a time of debt. *American Economic Review, 100*(2), 573–578.

Shaw, K. A. (2015). Breaching the welfare cap is actually good news for the Conservatives. *LSE British Politics and Policy Blog*, November 27. http://blogs.lse.ac.uk/politicsandpolicy/breaching-the-welfare-cap-is-actually-good-news-for-the-conservatives/. Accessed 2 Jan 2016.

Skidelsky, R. (2015a). George Osborne's cunning plan: How the chancellor's austerity narrative has harmed recovery. *New Statesman*, April 29. http://www.newstatesman.com/politics/2015/04/george-osborne-s-cunning-plan-how-chancellors-austerity-narrative-has-harmed. Accessed 10 Dec 2015.

Skidelsky, R. (2015b). The failure of austerity. Sheffield Political Economy Research Institute paper no. 23. http://speri.dept.shef.ac.uk/wp-content/uploads/2015/06/SPERIPaper23-the-failure-of-austerity.pdf. Accessed 10 Dec 2015.

Stanley, L. (2015a). Governing austerity in the UK. Paper presented at *Doing IPE*, University of Birmingham, 29 Nov 2015.
Stanley, L. (2015b). 'We're reaping what we sowed': Everyday crisis narratives and acquiescence to the age of austerity. *New Political Economy, 19*(6), 895–917.
Stanley, L. (2016). Legitimacy gaps, taxpayer conflict and the politics of austerity in the UK. *British Journal of Politics and International Relations*, forthcoming.
Streeck, W. (2014). Buying time: the delayed crisis of democratic capitalism. London: Verso.
Syal, R. (2015). 'Coin-toss chancellor' Osborne's 50/50 chance of meeting budget target. *The Guardian*, December 28. http://www.theguardian.com/business/2015/dec/28/coin-toss-chancellor-osborne-chance-meeting-spending-targets. Accessed 29 Dec 2015.
The Conservative Party. (2010). *An invitation to join the government of Britain: The conservative manifesto 2010.* http://media.conservatives.s3.amazonaws.com/manifesto/cpmanifesto2010_lowres.pdf. Accessed 9 Nov 2015.
The Conservative Party (2015). *Strong leadership, a clear economic plan, a brighter, more secure future.* https://www.conservatives.com/manifesto. Accessed 9 Nov 2015.
Tilly, G. (2015). Long term plan? Don't forget Osborne's sneaky 2014 spending boost. *Touchstone*, November 24. http://touchstoneblog.org.uk/2015/11/lets-not-forget-the-chancellors-low-key-but-significant-boost-to-spending-in-2014/. Accessed 10 Dec 2015.
Wolf, M. (2013). Austerity loses an article of faith. *The Financial Times*, April 23. http://www.ft.com/cms/s/0/60b7a4ec-ab58-11e2-8c63-00144feabdc0.html#axzz3wOICnFQG. Accessed 10 Dec 2015.
Wood, M., & Flinders, M. (2014). Rethinking depoliticisation: Beyond the governmental. *Policy & Politics, 42*(2), 151–170.
Wren-Lewis, S. (2015). The austerity con. *London Review of Books, 37*(4), 9–11.

CHAPTER 6

What's Left?

Abstract The main political opponents of the Conservative Party have struggled to develop a coherent set of ideas by which austerity may be challenged. Under Ed Miliband, the Labour Party struggled to construct an alternative to the pre-crisis growth model while accommodating austerity and, specifically, the perceived need for deficit reduction. The election of Jeremy Corbyn as Labour leader offers the prospect of a more coherent anti-austerity politics on the centre-left, yet there are few signs of austerity being dislodged from the the common sense of political discourse. The groups that seem to have had most success in challenging the Conservatives' ideological hegemony have been those that have strongly articulated localist or nationalist sentiment, yet these groups are pragmatic on economic policy and only opportunistically anti-austerity.

Keywords Social democracy • Left-wing politics • Austerity • Labour Party • Localism

Economic policy can never be considered the work of a single individual. Yet the preceding chapters have focused to an unusual extent on the vision and decisions of a single person, that is, George Osborne. The influence of other elite figures has been mentioned where relevant; it would be incongruous to deny the influence on UK economic policy over recent years of

C. Berry, *Austerity Politics and UK Economic Policy*, Building a Sustainable Political Economy: SPERI Research & Policy,
DOI 10.1057/978-1-137-59010-7_6

other leading members of the Conservative Party, most obviously David Cameron and, up to 2016, Iain Duncan Smith. Leading figures at the Bank of England and the Treasury have also helped to shape the apparent Osborne agenda, as did, up to 2015, leading Liberal Democrats such as Nick Clegg and Vince Cable. Many hands have shaped the austerity agenda personified in the form of Osborne. And yet—although there have been occasions where disagreements among elite figures have become apparent, and UK economic policy might have taken a slightly different shape had the distribution of power among policy elites been configured different—the period since 2010 must surely be characterised as one reflecting a remarkable degree of consensus among elite actors on the key elements of economic policy and how, more generally, to respond to the severe crisis of 2008. This is not to suggest that there are not important cleavages within the Conservative Party, notably over Europe (a debate which has been conducted in public and contributed to Iain Duncan Smith's resignation) and, to a lesser extent, immigration (where Cameron and Osborne still maintain a rhetorical commitment to curbing immigration, with little policy substance). Were the party's right to become ascendant, there would probably be policy differences which impinge upon economic policy. At root, however, the Eurosceptic position (within the Conservatives) is based on the view—accurate or otherwise—that EU membership has been a barrier to the defence of a lightly regulated domestic economy. Cameron and Osborne clearly agree, but believe that the benefits of unfettered access to European markets outweigh this problem. The recent emergence of the UK Independence Party (UKIP)—ostensibly a Eurosceptic party, but seemingly far more vexed about immigration—should also be noted in relation to these issues. However, there is little discord within the Conservative Party (and between the Conservative Party and UKIP) on the necessity of austerity and the wider economic policy agenda served by the austerity narrative.

There has certainly not existed the same degree of unity among those seeking to challenge the Conservative Party's approach to economic governance from the left since 2010, which is the focus of this chapter. Of course, leading Labour Party figures should be considered as part of the policy elite—it is only the conventions of democratic politics that demands they proclaim otherwise. As such, Labour's weak and largely incoherent response to austerity up to the 2015 general election could be said to arise from its quintessential acquiescence to austerity and the Osborne-led agenda, coupled with the necessity of appearing to oppose the coalition government on some aspects of its programme. However, this would be to dismiss too conclusively the possibility that many on the left and centre-left in the UK have genuinely sought, and continue to seek, transformation within the UK growth model, or alternatively, even if the details of what an alternative growth model might look like remain sketchy, understand that austerity is a self-defeating enterprise. This chapter looks first at the main, competing crisis-response narratives and positions evident within the Labour Party under Ed Miliband's leadership, before turning to the programme of his successor, Jeremy Corbyn. Finally, it considers the perspectives of other parties broadly located on the centre-left. The chapter argues that the significantly disparate nature of the varied perspectives on how (and why) austerity should be challenged is a demonstration of just how successful it has been as a governing philosophy.

Labour's Disorientation

It is widely acknowledged that the Brown government acted decisively in the wake of the financial crash of 2008, helping to avert the prospect of economic depression both domestically and, to some extent, globally. As such, the Labour Party in government acted to rescue the growth model that had essentially solidified under its stewardship from a near overnight collapse. Yet in ideological terms, Labour struggled to establish (or re-establish) its legitimacy as custodians of the growth model when confronted with the charge that their own profligacy in spending had caused the financial crisis and subsequent recession. Of course, the Blair and Brown governments cannot, by any reasonable measure, be characterised as profligate in terms of the public finances; in fact, their excessive caution about public spending, and more importantly, about making the case for public spending, probably contributed a great deal towards undermining Labour's credibility. The emergency measures enacted *after* autumn 2008, including a limited attempt at fiscal stimulus and an enormous increase in public debt, provided somewhat artificial evidence that fiscal policy *before* 2008 had been too reckless. The ideological resources did not exist within New Labour to challenge this emerging austerity narrative.

This dilemma has plagued the Labour Party ever since—contributing to the 2010 election defeat, but severely constraining any attempt at developing an anti-austerity narrative in opposition. The extent to which austerity changed the rules of the game became evident during the 2010 Labour leadership election. It is widely assumed that David Miliband *should* have won the contest—with only his brother Ed Miliband's support among the trade unions preventing a decisive victory. However, the differences in support for the two brothers among all three sections of the electoral college (the parliamentary party, individual members, and affiliated organisations [mainly trade unions]) were relatively insignificant. Ed Miliband did have a narrow lead among the unions, mirroring David Miliband's lead among parliamentarians, but owed his victory also to securing more of the transferred votes of individual party members (under the alternative vote electoral system), allowing him to decisively close down his brother's lead in this section after first-preference votes had been counted. Ultimately, more members supported David Miliband than Ed Miliband, but a very large number wanted anybody but David Miliband as leader—resulting in a rather astonishing defeat given that he had started the contest as the clear front runner as the 'heir to Blair', with the apparent 'Brownite' candidacy split between his brother and Ed Balls.

There should be little doubt that the failure of the 'Blairite' faction to regain the party leadership is related to the early success of the austerity narrative. The problem was not that David Miliband was either too pro-austerity, or too anti-austerity, but rather that he said remarkably little about fiscal policy (or economic policy more generally) during the leadership contest. He may, with better luck, have won the contest anyway. And his higher standing in public consciousness (given his lack of association with Gordon Brown) would in all likelihood have meant that Labour under his leadership would have represented a more challenging political opponent for Cameron and Osborne. It was clear to most parts of the labour movement, however, that David Miliband's ideological challenge to austerity would have been limited. Of course, in seeking to oppose rather than accommodate austerity, the Labour Party posed itself a series of intractable political dilemmas—precisely because austerity had been so successful, in such a short space of time, in enabling the ideological hegemony of the Conservative Party.

The need to respond to austerity left Labour with a choice between the strategies offered by the two Eds, even after Ed Miliband's leadership election victory. During his leadership campaign, Balls offered a sophisticated and passionate defence of a Keynesian approach to economic recovery, in a speech titled 'The case against the "growth deniers"', but more commonly known as 'the Bloomberg speech' (Balls 2010). He argued that the austerity agenda was premised on the idea that opportunities for strong economic growth were evaporating, therefore necessitating fiscal conservatism in order to ensure the public sector remained solvent, and able to respond when the next crisis hits. Balls argued, in contrast, that strong growth would be rekindled, therefore enabling a deficit reduction strategy led by higher tax revenues rather than spending cuts. It was a theme he further explored in a project with leading American economist (and economic policymaker) Larry Summers; Balls and Summers co-chaired the Commission on Inclusive Prosperity, which reported in early 2015 (Summers and Balls 2015). However, Balls did not succeed in embedding his approach in the Labour Party's response to austerity during this period. This is at least in part because he did not attempt to do so: Ed Balls and Ed Miliband had a fractious personal relationship, especially after 2010—exacerbated by the fact that Miliband originally chose the Blairite Alan Johnson to serve as his shadow chancellor, and only appointed Balls with some reluctance when Johnson resigned in 2011 (Pickard 2015). Balls appears to have disapproved, ostensibly from the right, of some Ed Miliband's attempts to question the norms of British capitalism (discussed further below), but also, ostensibly from the left, of Ed Miliband's focus on the implications of austerity rather than the agenda itself (Parker et al. 2014). It is also true, however, that Balls' own agenda became narrower and more conservative over time. Recognising the repeated failure of Osborne to meet his own deficit reduction targets, Balls concentrated on challenging the coalition government on the grounds of economic competence, rather than ideology. This was typified by his campaign to compel the OBR (discussed in the previous chapter) to assess the spending plans of opposition parties, as well as the government. He was determined to demonstrate that his plans were fiscally neutral in comparison to Osborne's, thereby nullifying the charge that Labour would overspend if re-elected. In the process, of course, his argument served to reinforce the sense that the OBR is the trusted arbiter of sound budget management—a sentiment that ultimately benefits the Conservative Party and rewards the pursuit of austerity. Above all, it seems, Balls recognised the limitations of seeking to contest something that had become incontestable—yet his proximity to the effectively demonised rule of Gordon Brown made it impossible for him to instead play Osborne at his own game.

Ed Miliband instead sought to 'change the conversation'. Yet in doing so, he was hampered consistently by the accusation that he did not take seriously the need to tackle the budget deficit. (In his 2014 conference speech, delivered from memory, Miliband forgot to deliver a passage on the deficit and budget responsibility [BBC News 2014].) Miliband introduced the notion of 'responsible capitalism' in 2011, arguing principally that the private sector practices should be more heavily regulated, but also making the case for corporate governance reform (Miliband 2011). He introduced the odd concept of '*pre*distribution' in 2012, in order to make the rather mundane argument that governments can and should shape how markets function—rather than simply seeking to *re*distribute the proceeds of growth when unfettered markets produce unequal outcomes (Miliband 2012). The latter hints at acquiescence to austerity, insofar as a more redistributive agenda would have more direct implications for fiscal policy, yet essentially both seek to reshape the intellectual territory upon which Labour sought to oppose the coalition government. In 2013, Miliband sought to challenge the Conservative agenda more directly, including public expenditure cuts, through highlighting what he called 'a cost of living crisis'. The associated promises included a higher minimum wage and more support for childcare (both of which the Conservative Party has appropriated to some extent), stronger controls on zero-hours contracts, and the repeal of some benefit cuts, most notably the bedroom tax (BBC News 2013).

Miliband was clearly comfortable in this territory, highlighting some of the daily struggles of ordinary people that coalition policy had caused or exacerbated. However, as suggested above, Miliband's attempt to address the consequences of austerity was not accompanied by any particular attempt to challenge austerity in a more fundamental sense. While he argued, quite persuasively, for change within the economy more generally, he was unable to confront directly the ultimate aim of the austerity agenda, that is, the retrenchment of the state's conventional fiscal role. As shadow work and pensions secretary, key Miliband ally Rachel Reeves led the campaign against the bedroom tax, yet immediately proclaimed upon promotion to the role in late 2013 that Labour would be 'tougher' than the Conservative on welfare recipients (cited in Helm 2013). Similarly, Miliband answered 'Hell yes!' when asked during the 2015 general election campaign if he felt he was tough enough to make the kind of cuts necessary to address the budget deficit (cited in Hawkins 2015). The overall result was a rather incoherent response from Miliband on the existential threat that austerity poses to social democracy; he adopted the banner of austerity when seemingly compelled to do so, yet with little credibility, and in a way that undermined his broader reform agenda. The quintessential problem was not of course how to respond to austerity, but rather what kind of alternative growth model Ed Miliband's Labour Party was actually pursuing. Ed Balls had initially offered a full-scale return to a version of the pre-crisis growth model, with a renewed role for Keynes-inspired public investment, before seemingly acknowledging that the ideological foundations of such an approach were relatively weak when viewed through the prism of austerity. Yet Ed Miliband made no serious attempt to outline what his alternative, more responsible version of capitalism (presumably with a smaller, or leaner, state) might actually look like in practice. This meant that Labour's answers to the pressing and unavoidable questions around austerity remained largely unsettled throughout Ed Miliband's leadership.

Ed Miliband took some inspiration from the 'Blue Labour' campaign, pursued under the political leadership of Jon Cruddas (2011) and intellectual guidance of Maurice Glasman (2011). Blue Labour originated in Glasman's activities on the fringes of the Labour Party in London, in the Citizens UK and living wage movements. Blue Labour's core agenda relates to concerns around identity, community, and tradition, based on a partial critique of New Labour for marginalising these issues in embracing both free markets and a managerialist state. Blue Labour has emphasised the importance of family, religious faith, and even love, in articulating how individuals can make meaningful contributions to society—a set of concerns which has led to a socially conservative position on some issues, but which Cruddas and Glasman insist (not entirely inaccurately) is grounded in early, pre-industrial socialist thought. As important as these issues are, they clearly do not form a coherent basis upon which institutionalised economic practice can be transformed. Indeed, even Blue Labour's support for the living wage is couched predominantly in an understanding of how low pay tends to problematise community life, rather than in a critique of the UK growth model, and Cruddas' embrace of Englishness as a political identity is, above all, focused on issues around belonging and constitutional recognition rather than economic renewal at the subnational level (see Cruddas 2015a). Both Cruddas and Glasman were close to Ed Miliband during his leadership, with Cruddas appointed to lead Labour's policy review in 2012. The problem is that Blue Labour offered no substantive position on austerity or any macroeconomic issues.

The group's instinctive aversion to the state in fact means that elements of the austerity agenda fit fairly comfortably within a Blue Labour perspective, even if they would reject the individualism which underpins the Conservative Party's anti-state orientation. While rejecting the opportunity to comment on the economic soundness of austerity, Cruddas' independent review of Labour's election defeat (having resigned from the shadow cabinet after the election) identified Miliband's anti-austerity position as the chief culprit, based on some fairly unscientific polling evidence. Cruddas commissioned polling company YouGov to ask voters whether they agreed with the statement: 'We must live within our means, so cutting the deficit is the top priority' (Cruddas 2015b)—clearly a rather forceful form of words, at odds with the open questions that YouGov has routinely been asking voters since 2010, which usually produce around double the number of 'disagree' responses on whether austerity (or deficit reduction) is necessary (Stanley 2015). As such, Cruddas sought to offer sustenance to an emerging pro-austerity narrative emanating from the right of the Labour Party. As noted above, the so-called Blairite faction had said little about austerity or fiscal issues more generally in the wake of the 2010 election defeat. (Interestingly, discomfort with his economic policy brief was one of the reasons [alongside some personal problems] that Alan Johnson resigned from his role as shadow chancellor after only a few months.) The case for fiscal conservatism was made by some associated with the party in 2012, under the banner of 'Black Labour' (mean to signify that Labour could deliver social justice while the public finances remained 'in the black') (Cooke et al. 2011; Lent et al. 2013). However, this perspective found no major advocate until the 2015 leadership campaign, when it was forcefully taken up by Liz Kendall. Kendall ended up with fewer than 5 per cent of first-preference votes among individual members and registered supporters (under a reformed election model). The question of whether Kendall would have proved far more popular with the wider electorate than within her own party may be a fascinating counterfactual, but largely irrelevant to understanding the politics of austerity. The more significant conclusion is that the success of austerity makes contesting the perceived centre ground extremely difficult for anybody but its natural adherents within the conservative ideological tradition. Kendall was not appealing to this group, but rather a group of people significantly hardened against the idea of accommodating austerity, precisely because they recognised its inherently conservative and neoliberal connotations, even if it were to be pursued through the centre-left.

Corbynomics and the New Old Politics

In this context, Labour's radical shift leftwards, in electing the 'Bennite' Jeremy Corbyn to succeed Ed Miliband in 2015, seems almost inevitable. The fact that austerity has demonised the means of pursuing social democratic goals has encouraged a significant majority of traditional Labour activists and supporters to seek to reject austerity *de jure*, even if the potential electoral dividend is not immediately apparent. Once Corbyn got onto the ballot for the leadership contest, he quickly amassed enough support to win, even benefiting from his own apparent reluctance to stand, insofar as it demonstrated his modest character (even if this impression of Corbyn is accurate, it would certainly not apply to his shadow chancellor John McDonnell, a perennial leadership candidate who would probably have stood in Corbyn's place if either believed that he could have won). It has to be pointed out that Corbyn's victory was, to some extent, accidental. Firstly, he had to secure the nomination of 35 Labour MPs to become a candidate, and only did so after a large number of MPs that did not support his candidacy chose to nominate him in order to broaden the subsequent debates. Secondly, even though he won a decisive majority among full party members, he benefited greatly from the support of 'registered supporters', who were able to acquire a vote in the leadership contest in return for a one-off payment of £3, under a model introduced by Ed Miliband (and strongly supported, at the time, on the right of the party). It is fair to assume that Corbyn's victory would have been much more difficult, or impossible, had the party elite made different decisions on both issues. However, while this is, again, a fascinating counterfactual, it is not a conclusion that helps us to understand the politics of austerity across the ideological spectrum in the UK. The fact is that the party elite did make some naïve decisions, not because of any cognitive deficiency, but rather because they completely failed to understand the attitudinal change that austerity represents. Corbyn's victory could not have been predicted by Cameron and Osborne, but it is nevertheless a product of the disorientation within Labour ranks that austerity is designed in part to engender.

Corbyn's long career as a backbencher has been devoted primarily to foreign policy issues. However, in tandem with McDonnell, he has also long sought to resist the Labour Party's accommodation to neoliberalism after the 1983 election defeat, promoting instead the economic policy agenda outlined in the 1983 manifesto, for substantial public investment through a state-led industrial policy, nationalisation of key firms including financial institutions, high levels of taxation to enable wealth redistribution, and tighter controls on capital movement, prices, and imports. However, there is relatively little evidence that Corbyn and McDonnell intend, or are able, to pursue such a radical agenda in the near future. The 'alternative economic strategy', developed by Marxist thinkers in the 1970s, which inspired the politics of Michael Foot, Tony Benn, and Ken Livingstone (in his first incarnation as the leader of the Greater London Council in the 1980s), was essentially a critique of Keynesian political economy, and yet Corbyn and McDonnell are not yet offering a policy agenda that would look out of place in a fairly mainstream Keynesian programme, which could quite easily have been articulated by Ed Balls had he further developed his Bloomberg speech agenda (Gamble 2015).

McDonnell's main demand appears to be that central government should significantly increase levels of public investment, funded through borrowing. He has indicated support for a national investment bank and, most intriguingly, suggested a programme of 'people's quantitative easing' (PQE). PQE would operate similarly to QE, as discussed in the second chapter, only the Bank of England would be buying new bonds issued by a national investment bank, rather than repurchasing government bonds from private actors. PQE would therefore enable the government to 'print money' to directly stimulate the 'real economy', rather than relying on the stimulus to be filtered through capital markets. Other stated policy aims include the renationalisation of the railway industry (with a proposed renationalisation of energy suppliers now seemingly shelved) and greater financial regulation (albeit with little detail on what this might entail). Corbyn and McDonnell continue to support higher levels of taxation on wealthy individuals and corporations, but this agenda is generally only articulated now as an alternative means of deficit reduction, rather than as a pillar of redistribution (Corbyn 2015b; McDonnell 2015). As such, Andrew Gamble (2015) has commented insightfully that 'Corbynomics may share many of the biases of the alternative economic strategy, but as yet it is only a very pale reflection of it as an economic programme'. The problem, however, especially in relation to austerity, should perhaps be stated in reverse. Corbyn and McDonnell offer a mildly Keynesian programme rather than a radical challenge to capitalism, yet their agenda is interpreted, or depicted, as extremely radical, to the point of being rather 'un-British'. Of course, Corbyn would have to go some distance to match the radicalism and novelty of George Osborne's macroeconomic policy agenda, outlined in the second chapter; indeed, while Osborne's endorsement of austerity prevents him from borrowing to invest to any significant degree, or establishing a meaningful national investment bank, the adoption of PQE in some form by the Conservative Party in the event of another severe economic downturn is not particularly difficult to imagine. Versions of PQE have in fact been advocated by key establishment figures such as Adair Turner (former head of the Financial Services Authority) and Adam Posen (former member of the Bank of England's Monetary Policy Committee) (Klein 2015). However, whereas PQE would be depicted by the Conservative government as a purely technocratic adjustment, in the hands of Jeremy Corbyn, so the argument goes, it would represent a dangerous and self-indulgent profligacy.

Corbyn's success within the Labour Party undoubtedly signifies a longing for an alternative to austerity on the left, but he is not offering a particularly concrete alternative to the pre-crisis growth model. Corbyn and McDonnell want to invest a great deal more, but their thoughts on where this investment might be directed are, at best, sketchy. McDonnell was widely ridiculed for describing his industrial policy agenda as 'socialism with an iPad' (Wintour 2015)—a crude attempt to demonstrate his appreciation of the transformation that has occurred within capitalist production in recent decades. Such moves are of course undermined by Corbyn's declaration of support for reopening coal mines during the leadership contest (another policy which was quickly jettisoned after his victory, and yet which will probably linger in public consciousness) (Wearmouth 2015). One of the strangest aspects of the Corbyn and McDonnell macroeconomic agenda is that they do not appear to have a settled position on austerity, or more precisely, how to respond to austerity. In essence, they would simply like to ignore the discourse around austerity, on the basis that, in Corbyn's words, 'Labour shouldn't be swallowing the story that austerity is anything other than a new facade for the same Tory plans' (Corbyn 2015b, p. 3). This was the slightly dismissive rhetoric offered by Corbyn in the leadership contest, and although he is broadly justified in identifying austerity as a smokescreen for the continuation of financialisation and a neoliberal economic policy agenda, the problem is that austerity simply cannot be dismissed. Its macroeconomic erroneousness is irrelevant; Corbyn, hailing from a radical fringe of the labour movement, is even less able than Ed Miliband to 'change the conversation', yet the notion that he might win a general election without confronting Osbornomics directly is a rather fantastical one.

Corbyn and McDonnell's incoherent contribution to austerity politics was typified by a bizarre incident in late 2015, when McDonnell signalled support for Osborne's statutory fiscal charter, as discussed in the previous chapter. McDonnell had evidently wanted to convey the message that Labour was serious about, and capable of, reducing the budget deficit, through enabling strong growth rather than cutting spending. Ironically, this position enabled the new leadership to postpone a showdown with the advocates of austerity on the Labour benches. However, it seems that the political implications of promising to balance the capital budget by 2020—when most of Labour's growth-inducing measures depended upon much higher levels of public investment—only became clear to McDonnell several days later. Labour's position was quickly reversed to one of strong opposition to the charter. Moreover, the activist group Momentum, which originated from Corbyn's leadership campaign, explicitly threatened to pursue the deselection of any Labour MP that voted with the government (in the event, 21 Labour MPs abstained on the charter) (Bush 2015).

Whither Social Democracy?

It is clear that austerity is a serious and potentially existential challenge to the traditional social democratic orientation dominant on the UK centre-left, due essentially to the demonisation of the prospect of public authorities to use fiscal policy to pursue collective goods. The notion of shared, societal responsibility has been problematised by the valorisation of the need for individuals to be self-sufficient. This section briefly considers the role of parties other than Labour in the politics of austerity in the UK.

The Liberal Democrats have of course been mentioned several times throughout this book, reflecting their role as a junior coalition partner—yet it is reasonable to conclude that they exercised relatively little influence on the core elements of the Conservatives' austerity agenda. At the 2015 general election, the party fell into a version of the trap which also ensnared Ed Miliband, promising to maintain austerity but implement it in a fairer manner. After Nick Clegg's resignation, however, the party elected Tim Farron from the left of the party—Farron had often publicly criticised the Liberal Democrats' role in the coalition government and in pursuing austerity. Of course, the election of Jeremy Corbyn as Labour leader pulls the rug from under Farron's feet to some extent (the party had evidently expected Labour to move back towards the perceived centre, enabling Farron to assume the mantle of the late Charles Kennedy, who often positioned the party to the left of the Blair government). However, it is not at all clear that the electorate would have warmed to Farron's more left-wing approach anyway, any more than they appear to be warming to Corbyn's Labour. While the Liberal Democrats were pilloried for collaborating with the Conservatives in government, their disastrous performance at the 2015 election (when they were reduced from 55 to 8 seats in the House of Commons) was due far more to a loss of support to the Conservative Party to the right, than to Labour or any other party to the left. Insofar as a post-coalition renaissance for the Liberal Democrats is at all likely, its strongest prospects probably lie in seeking to develop the localist politics that Clegg began to pursue in office (as discussed in Chap. 3). While austerity reframes what it means for advocates of liberalism to protect individual freedom, it also perhaps opens up opportunities for individuals to demand more meaningful control over policy decisions within their communities if they are to be expected to demonstrate a greater degree of self-sufficiency. As such, a localist turn may have given the Liberal Democrats an opportunity to oppose the implications of austerity in a fairly novel way without seeming to dismantle their own record in delivering austerity in office. Alas, it is not apparent that Farron is willing or able to engage with this form of politics with any authority, insofar as his support derives from those eager for the Liberal Democrats to challenge Osbornomics directly within the national arena. He is talented and sincere enough to win some battles in this regard, and the party will surely recover from its extremely low ebb—but winning the war is a very dim prospect.

The potential of a more localist—even parochial—political narrative as an effective response to austerity is demonstrated by the recent success of the Scottish National Party (SNP) in Scotland. The SNP won a majority in the Scottish parliamentary election of 2011, and then 56 of 59 Scottish seats in the 2015 general election (having previously held only 6). In September 2014, Scotland voted to remain as part of the UK—but far more narrowly than had been anticipated only a few months before. The SNP has used anti-austerity rhetoric very effectively in positioning itself to the left of Labour in Scotland, identifying austerity as a key example of Westminster misrule, and demanding additional powers to enable the SNP to manage Scotland's economy in a fairer manner. However, there is considerable doubt as to whether the SNP offers a genuinely anti-austerity position. Analysis by both the Institute for Fiscal Studies (IFS) (Crawford et al. 2015) and Resolution Foundation (Kelly and Corlett 2015) suggests that the differences between the SNP and, for instance, the Labour Party in terms of their spending commitments in advance of the 2015 general election were relatively minor. This is especially odd given that the SNP had no chance of forming the UK government in 2015 and, even if they had joined a Labour-led coalition in some form, would not have expected to be held to their manifesto commitments in these circumstances. So why adopt a fairly strict deficit reduction plan? It seems clear that the SNP is eager to be seen as fiscally conservative, even if its exclusive focus on Scottish politics offers a licence to eschew the actual term 'austerity' to some extent. As James Stafford (2015) has argued, the SNP offers only a moderately progressive economic policy agenda, endowed with pragmatism, broadly similar to New Labour in its focus on macroeconomic stability and supply-side reforms. For David Torrance (2015), the SNP's success lies in its embodiment of the sense than Scotland can do things—even if 'very often the same things'—for itself.

There is some evidence of localist sentiment becoming more popular within Northern England, including through the establishment of localist or regionalist parties identifying with and organising at various geographical scales. These parties are united by 'a critique of austerity and its local impact', but are generally located around the centre of the ideological spectrum in terms of economic policy (Cox and Giovannini 2015, p. 54). Localist parties in the North do not appear to have entertained the possibility of advocating secession from the UK, yet their emergence is clearly part of the same dynamic, intensified by the financial crisis, that has propelled the SNP to greater electoral success in Scotland. Moreover, it would probably not be inaccurate to suggest that local sections of the Labour Party are becoming more localist in their outlook, as evidenced by a widespread willingness among Labour's civic leaders in the North to co-operate with George Osborne's Northern Powerhouse agenda (Blakely and Evans 2015). They will of course publicly criticise austerity, acutely aware of the impact of spending cuts on local government, but appear relatively comfortable making deals with Osborne if it means that some economic powers will be devolved to the local or regional level. This does not mean that local Labour Party leaders are unaware of the limitations of the Northern Powerhouse agenda as a form of decentralisation, yet this awareness only serves to underline the pragmatism that typifies the approach of many Labour local government leaders now. Austerity is disliked, but it is not considered an insurmountable barrier to achieving greater prosperity within local economies, and although none of the actors pursuing varying degrees of a localist agenda in UK post-crisis politics would articulate their strategies in these terms, it seems clear that they are to some extent reinforcing austerity as the Conservative Party understand it, by proclaiming their ability to prosper with lower levels of fiscal support from central government. Tellingly, the divergence between centre and local within the Labour Party has already impacted upon Jeremy Corbyn as leader (the third chapter noted Corbyn's remark that the Northern Powerhouse is 'a cruel deception'), as local leaders expressed dismay at the national party's opposition to the Conservative government's Cities and Local Government Devolution Bill in October 2015, which was shaped in large part by the deals struck between the Treasury and Labour-led local authorities (Harrison 2015; Jones 2015). Of course, only time will tell if the pragmatic parochialism that characterises, to some extent, local Labour Party politics will prove more electorally attractive than Corbyn's agenda at the national level.

It is worth commenting, finally, on the Green Party, which to some extent challenges what it means to be centre-left, insofar as its politics is not primarily about responding to capitalism, or centred around collective action through the state, and as such neither the financial crisis nor austerity have been hugely disruptive to the party's extant narratives. Its core concerns nevertheless chime with some of the concerns reflected in support for Jeremy Corbyn, and in substantive terms, the Greens were the only large party to reject deficit reduction as a short-term fiscal objective in 2015. The Green Party improved its share of the vote between the 2010 and 2015 elections from 1 per cent to 4 per cent (although it did not add to its single seat in the Commons). However, the potential centrality of green ideas to the centre-left in UK politics remains far from realisation. This may be because it has largely eschewed the opportunity to articulate its concern in relation to the localist sentiment that characterises responses to austerity elsewhere on the centre-left. The Green Party essentially treats climate change as a universal threat; although this may be accurate, from a scientific perspective, it renders the party's *raison d'être* rather abstract. There has seemingly been little attempt to describe environmental change through the discursive prism of place, emphasising the threat of climate change to our physical security and everyday life in local areas. An additional problem for the Green Party is that criticising individual behaviour forms such an integral part of its politics (insofar as individuals contribute to waste and overconsumption). The instinctive appeal of this narrative is probably superseded by the austerity-derived imperative for individuals to behave more selfishly. The Green Party overwhelmingly seeks to use the tax system to enforce behavioural change by individuals and private enterprises; it will probably become more popular among some groups in the near future as a radical alternative to austerity, but at the same time, it is reasonable to assume that the views of the majority might have begun to harden against the party.

Conclusion

Austerity has seemingly disabled many of the traditional means and ends of social democracy in the UK. One of the principal beneficiaries has been an apparent rise in localist sentiment, albeit to vastly different degrees in different areas. Localist actors often position themselves in opposition to an austerity agenda driven from the centre, but are essentially pragmatic on most areas of economic policy—even indifferent when it comes to major macroeconomic policy debates. We are certainly seeing evidence of a willingness among a large portion of the electorate to mobilise in favour of a more radical economic policy agenda, typified by the election of Jeremy Corbyn as Labour Party leader. Yet in seeking to construct a governing coalition, Corbyn has had to seek to accommodate those within the parliamentary party more sympathetic to the need to reduce the budget deficit in the short term, and indeed to demonstrate his understanding of public concerns about Labour's perceived profligacy. However, the end result is to entangle his agenda in the same dilemmas that paralysed his predecessor Ed Miliband. Local Labour Party representatives appear to be learning from the SNP that it is much easier to maintain an anti-austerity position when you are absolved of any meaningful responsibility for challenging it at the national level.

References

Balls, E. (2010). The case against 'growth deniers'. Speech delivered on 27 August 2010. https://www.youtube.com/watch?v=TqER8CPtCiI. Accessed 13 Nov 2015.

BBC News. (2013, 21 September). Labour: Miliband outlines 'cost of living crisis' plans. http://www.bbc.co.uk/news/uk-24184473. Accessed 13 Nov 2015.

BBC News. (2014, 24 September). Ed Miliband forgets deficit and immigration in speech. http://www.bbc.co.uk/news/uk-politics-29339581. Accessed 13 Nov 2015.

Blakeley, G., & Evans, B. (2015, November 12). An idea whose time has come? Explaining the (sudden) emergence of Devo-Manc. Paper presented at *The political economy of the Northern Powerhouse*, University of Sheffield.

Bush, S. (2015). Labour MPs are worried about Momentum. Should they be? *The Staggers*, October 26. http://www.newstatesman.com/politics/staggers/2015/10/labour-mps-are-worried-about-momentum-should-they-be. Accessed 13 Nov 2015.

Cooke, G., Lent, A., Painter, A., & Sen, H. (2011). *In the black labour: Why fiscal conservatism and social justice go hand-in-hand, policy network*. http://www.policy-network.net/publications/4101/-In-the-black-Labour. Accessed 13 Nov 2015.

Corbyn, J. (2015a). *Northern future*. https://d3n8a8pro7vhmx.cloudfront.net/jeremyforlabour/pages/103/attachments/original/1438626641/NorthernFuture.pdf?1438626641. Accessed 8 Nov 2015.

Corbyn, J. (2015b). *The economy in 2020*. http://www.solidariteetprogres.org/IMG/pdf/theeconomyin2020_jeremycorbyn-220715.pdf. Accessed 13 Nov 2015.

Cox, E., & Giovannini, A. (2015). Northern voices: How far can a bottom-up 'new regionalism' go towards answering the English question? *Juncture, 22*(1), 52–57.

Crawford, R., Emmerson, C., Keynes, S., Tetlow, G. (2015). Post-election austerity: Parties' plans compared. Institute for Fiscal Studies Briefing Note no. 170. http://www.ifs.org.uk/uploads/publications/bns/BN170.pdf. Accessed 18 Nov 2015.

Cruddas, J. (2011). A country for old men. *New Statesman*, April 7. http://www.newstatesman.com/uk-politics/2011/04/english-labour-tradition. Accessed 13 Nov 2015.

Cruddas, J. (2015a). Labour is lost in England. *LabourList*, September 22. http://labourlist.org/2015/09/jon-cruddas-labour-is-lost-in-england/. Accessed 13 Nov 2015.

Cruddas, J. (2015b). Labour lost because voters believed it was anti-austerity. *LabourList*, August 5. http://labourlist.org/2015/08/labour-lost-because-voters-believed-it-was-anti-austerity/. Accessed 13 Nov 2015.

Gamble, A. (2015). Although sharing many of the biases of the 'alternative economic strategy' developed on the left in Britain in the 1970s and 1980s, Corbyn's economic programme is as yet no more than a pale reflection of the ideas of that era. *SPERI Comment*, November 3. http://speri.dept.shef.ac.uk/2015/11/03/corbynomics-part-1/. Accessed 13 Nov 2015.

Glasman, M. (2011). My blue labour vision can defeat the coalition. *The Guardian*, April 24. http://www.theguardian.com/politics/2011/apr/24/blue-labour-maurice-glasman. Accessed 13 Nov 2015.

Harrison, B. (2015). Labour's response to the Cities Bill: an unreasonable 'reasoned amendment', Centre for Cities. http://www.centreforcities.org/blog/labours-response-to-the-cities-bill-an-unreasonable-reasoned-amendment/. Accessed 18 Nov 2015.

Hawkins, R. (2015). Analysis: 'Hell yes, I'm tough enough to be PM'. *BBC News*, March 27. http://www.bbc.co.uk/news/uk-32080184. Accessed 13 Nov 2015.

Helm, T. (2013). Labour will be tougher than Tories on benefits, promises new welfare chief. *The Observer*, October 13. http://www.theguardian.com/politics/2013/oct/12/labour-benefits-tories-labour-rachel-reeves-welfare. Accessed 13 Nov 2015.

Jones, A. (2015). Three big questions about labour's stance on devolution. *City Metric*, October 5. http://www.citymetric.com/politics/three-big-questions-about-labour-s-stance-devolution-1458. Accessed 18 Nov 2015.

Kelly, G. and Corlett, A. (2015). "The SNP and austerity: how different are they to the other parties?", *Resolution Foundation*. http://www.resolutionfoundation.org/media/blog/the-snp-and-austerity-how-different-are-they-to-the-other-parties/. Accessed 18 Nov 2015.

Klien, M. (2015). Corbyn's 'people's QE' could actually be a decent idea. *FT Alphaville*, August 6. http://ftalphaville.ft.com/2015/08/06/2136475/corbyns-peoples-qe-could-actually-be-a-decent-idea/. Accessed 13 Nov 2015.

Lent, A., Sen, H., & Painter, A. (2013). *Moving labour 'into the black'*. Policy Network. http://www.policy-network.net/pno_detail.aspx?ID=4422&title=Moving-Labour-%E2%80%98into-the-black-. Accessed 13 Nov 2015.

McDonnell, J. (2015). Party conference speech. Speech delivered on 28 September 2015. http://press.labour.org.uk/post/130055656854/speech-by-john-mcdonnell-to-labour-party-annual. Accessed 13 Nov 2015.

Miliband, E. (2011). Speech on a new economy. Speech delivered on 17 November 2011. http://www.newstatesman.com/economy/2011/11/term-business-government. Accessed 13 Nov 2015.

Miliband, E. (2012). Predistribution speech. Speech delivered on 6 September 2012.http://www.politics.co.uk/comment-analysis/2012/09/06/ed-miliband-s-redistribution-speech-in-full. Accessed 13 Nov 2015.

Parker, G., Pickard, J., & Groom, B. (2014). UK politics: Labour and the City. *The Financial Times*, June 12. http://www.ft.com/cms/s/0/3a98788a-efc8-11e3-9b4c-00144feabdc0.html#axzz3sPTpO2pJ. Accessed 13 Nov 2015.

Pickard, J. (2015). Miliband faces dilemma over chancellor choice. *The Financial Times*, March 30. http://www.ft.com/cms/s/0/25b93276-d247-11e4-9c25-00144feab7de.html#axzz3sPTpO2pJ. Accessed 13 Nov 2015.

Stafford, J. (2015). The revenge of sovereignty: The SNP, financial crisis and UK constitutional reform. Sheffield Political Economy Research Institute paper no. 20. http://speri.dept.shef.ac.uk/wp-content/uploads/2015/03/Paper-20-The-Revenge-of-Sovereignty.pdf. Accessed 18 Nov 2015.

Stanley, L. (2015). What six public opinion graphs tell us about austerity. *SPERI Comment*, July 9. http://speri.dept.shef.ac.uk/2015/07/09/public-opinion-graphs-austerity/. Accessed 13 Nov 2015.

Summers, L., & Balls, E. (2015). *Report on the Commission on inclusive prosperity*. Center for American Progress. https://www.americanprogress.org/issues/economy/report/2015/01/15/104266/report-of-the-commission-on-inclusive-prosperity/. Accessed 13 Nov 2015.

Torrance, D. (2015). The reinvention of the SNP. *The Guardian*, May 21. http://www.theguardian.com/politics/2015/may/21/how-alex-salmond-nicola-sturgeon-pulled-off-political-triumph-lifetime. Accessed 18 Nov 2015.

Wearmouth, R. (2015). Labour leadership frontrunner Jeremy Corbyn vows to reopen coal mines if he becomes Prime Minister. *The Mirror*, August 9. http://www.mirror.co.uk/news/uk-news/labour-leadership-frontrunner-jeremy-corbyn-6221443. Accessed 13 Nov 2015.

Wintour, P. (2015). John McDonnell to unveil 'socialism with an iPad' economic plan. *The Guardian*, November 20. http://www.theguardian.com/politics/2015/nov/20/john-mcdonnell-to-unveil-socialism-with-an-ipad-economic-plan. Accessed 21 Nov 2015.

CHAPTER 7

Conclusion

Abstract The financial crisis undoubtedly represented a moment of upheaval in the UK economy. However, the elite-level ideational response it produced was not novel, but rather drew upon extant traditions of thought, most obviously those associated with the notion of austerity. As such, the crisis has been defined in accordance with the perspectives and interests of some groups rather than others, drawing upon certain values and assumptions about economic life that pertain irrespective of the proximity of crisis. In short, austerity promises 'radical continuity' in economic statecraft. Yet we should not assume that the hegemony of this position will persist indefinitely; austerity is an idea for exceptional times, and it remains unclear whether acquiescence to its prescriptions will continue in more 'normal' political and economic circumstances.

Keywords Crisis • Growth • Austerity • Ideas • Hegemony

Austerity and Crisis

Mark Blyth's *Austerity: The History of a Dangerous Idea* (2013) remains perhaps the most important work on austerity in the field of political economy since the financial crisis. Blyth's historical and comparative approach enables him to demonstrate that austerity in the contemporary era is highly

C. Berry, *Austerity Politics and UK Economic Policy*, Building a Sustainable Political Economy: SPERI Research & Policy,
DOI 10.1057/978-1-137-59010-7_7

unlikely to enable strong economic growth—because it never has in the past. Austerity, for Blyth, is about making the poor pay for the mistakes of the rich, that is, an excessive concentration of wealth in too few hands, producing pathologies which invariably result in economic crises, typically financial crises. This book has not sought to depart from Blyth's understanding of austerity for the most part, rather to add to it with an explication of how austerity has been applied in the UK. This additional layer of policy detail, however, enables the book to reflect upon how the advocates of austerity expect individuals to respond to austerity, or more profoundly, to live in an austere age. More importantly, while Blyth considers the role of austerity in suppressing growth, from a broadly Keynesian perspective, this book asks instead how the pursuit of austerity in the UK sustains a specific *growth model*, which is ostensibly organised around the pursuit of economic growth, albeit by particular means.

Blyth's account of austerity is also hampered by an ambiguity regarding the ontological status of ideational phenomena, such as austerity, in relation to economic crises—the same ambiguity that is present in Blyth's earlier work on crises and ideas. In *Great Transformations*, Blyth argues that the interests of agents, including elites, are not derived rationally from a perceived set of material and structural circumstances, but rather constructed via the prism of the paradigmatic 'economic ideas' that dominate a particular epoch. However, he subsequently argues that these economic ideas are invalidated at moments of crisis—and the crisis is only resolved when new economic ideas emanating from 'key economic actors' (such as organised business groups) are institutionalised (Blyth 2002, pp. 9, 10). The implication is that, at this moment, key economic actors are able to perceive their real, unfiltered interests, and accordingly develop new ideas which enable the establishment of a new order to suit these interests; it is, at root, a materialist account of economic history (see Hay 2002). In a sense, austerity fits the profile of an economic idea applied at a time of crisis to serve the interests of the powerful and resourceful. Yet it is not a new idea. Moreover, although the word itself may not have been in vogue within political discourse, it rests upon ideas related to fiscal conservatism and individual responsibility which were very much present in the immediate pre-crisis period.

It is certainly the case that some groups have a much stronger interest in sustaining a modified version of the pre-crisis growth model than others. Yet it is precisely this recognition that austerity underpins the resurrection of the extant growth model, not the development of a new economic order, that should caution us against any simplistic account of how ideas are used in the aftermath of economic crises. Blyth's work on crises sought to account for the emergence of neoliberalism as a new economic idea (or set of ideas) in the 1970s. But his more recent work on the history of austerity shows that, despite frequent crises, the development of capitalist economies is best considered as a process of evolution rather than a series of revolutions. Accordingly, we must take care when assigning descriptors such as 'crisis' to moments of apparent upheaval. It is of course correct to identify moments of genuine crisis within capitalist development, as long as we maintain the possibility that some crises are fabricated for political purposes, that a crisis for some groups may be experienced very differently by others, and that the extent and definition of particular crises are always the subjects of political struggle. As an idea invoked in the wake of perceived crises, the meaning of austerity changes, subtly, over time, and in different political and economic contexts. But it is not reinvented anew each time elites' apparent interests are fundamentally at risk. It is ultimately the product of certain values and assumptions (regarding markets, individuality, property, money, etc.) which pertain to economic life—particularly in the UK—irrespective of the proximity of crisis.

The UK Growth Model

The meaning of austerity in post-crisis UK is a subtle variation on what the term might have meant at certain points in the past. It certainly has implications for the state, but it signifies primarily a need for individuals to shoulder a greater degree of responsibility for their own lives. The state must become smaller in order to facilitate individual self-sufficiency. It is implied in turn that such an arrangement better enables the economy to function in accordance with free-market logic. Of course, the state under austerity has actually become enlarged in some ways, but usually only to help to create or restore certain market-based regimes, or encourage individuals to participate in the market following the retraction of traditional state functions.

However, we should not confuse the discursive implications of austerity with the objectives of the pursuit of austerity as a governing strategy. The austerity narrative is promulgated, chiefly by the Conservative Party, to justify the resurrection of the UK's pre-crisis growth model, insofar as it serves as the underlying rationale for a series of policy measures in the vein of 'radical continuity'. These measures directly benefit the finance sector and the housing market, facilitate the perpetuation of a consumption-led economy based on personal debt (rather than a genuine industrial renaissance enabled by greater levels of long-term investment) and, more indirectly, support the growth of low-pay service industries. As such, the growth model supported by policy elites in the post-crisis period sustains patterns of wealth distribution similar to those which pertained in the pre-crisis period, albeit with inequality arguably more pronounced as financial and property wealth remains largely intact while earnings are held down and redistributive mechanisms are withdrawn.

Austerity serves the dual purpose of diagnosing the crisis and prescribing the response. Clearly, as discussed in the introductory chapter, although growth models are about much more than growth, they must ostensibly be geared towards delivering economic growth. As such, the pre-crisis growth model could not have been rescued had the crisis been widely interpreted as one *of growth*. Austerity redefines the crisis as one of public debt and, quintessentially, of the state (or, more precisely, of the wrong kind of state). The state's role as an employer and investor in public services—an important element of the pre-crisis model—has therefore been scaled back in the post-crisis period, both to contribute to public debt reduction, but also to avoid polluting austerity's ideological agenda. The coalition and Conservative governments have of course occasionally reconsidered this dimension of austerity when the consequences for the economic recovery have proved particularly problematic, but they have done so as quietly as possible. Their apparent defence of the healthcare budget is not a contradiction, but rather an exception that proves the rule, as a *de jure* championing of the National Health Service (NHS) underlines how little the Conservative Party values the rest of the public sector.

The delegitimisation of the collectivist state decimates the traditional foundation of left and centre-left politics in the UK. Some parts of the left have consciously adopted an anti-austerity stance, albeit with great difficulty. Localist, regionalist, and nationalist sentiment has grown in popularity on the left in recent years, with some electoral success, and a growing political influence more generally, although this trend does not represent a direct threat to austerity, and may even reinforce the logic of self-sufficiency beyond the collectivist state. Crucially, the Conservative Party has quite effectively appropriated traditionally leftist political agendas in some regards, such as boosting underperforming regions in the North of England. However, they are pursuing such objectives almost exclusively through market mechanisms or through promoting private enterprise. Where, in the past, the limitations of such strategies might have been scrutinised, the decline of the state's legitimacy in public discourse ensures that their credibility is now largely unquestioned.

And Finally

Is it possible to conclude with any certainty on what this period represents in the development of the UK economy and economic statecraft? We may of course be living through a 'morbid interregnum' in Gramscian terms, with the dissolution of the old order not yet complete, but nevertheless inevitable. The absence of confusion (with the exception of the UK's EU membership) among policy elites suggests otherwise—we have witnessed decisive and purposeful political action in this regard, led by the Conservative Party in government. However, this does not mean that the resurrected order is impervious to being blown off course by any number of storms gathering domestically and internationally, in ways that elites would now find difficult to manage. And the fact that large parts of the labour movement have now withdrawn their tacit support for growth model resurrection is some indication of an unruly future. It is also worth noting that the Conservative Party's ideological hegemony has not been translated into electoral dominance; the party won a majority in the 2015 election, but on an unusually small vote share. Austerity may be tolerated as necessary evil, but it is loved by few. One thing we do know with a greater degree of certainty, therefore, is that economic statecraft in the UK cannot continue to use the 2008 financial crisis as a legitimising pillar indefinitely. As an idea, austerity is perennial, but only really functions as a response to crisis. Austerity is not in itself a permanent way of economic life, and the economic order that it seeks to defend and promote must develop new ways of justifying its existence eventually, including in a clear demonstration of its ability to create genuine prosperity.

References

Blyth, M. (2002). *Great transformations: Economic ideas and institutional change in the twentieth century*. Cambridge: Cambridge University Press.

Blyth, M. (2013). *Austerity: The history of a dangerous idea*. Oxford: Oxford University Press.

Hay, C. (2002). *Political analysis*. Basingstoke: Palgrave MacMillan.

Index

C. Berry, *Austerity Politics and UK Economic Policy*, Building a Sustainable Political Economy: SPERI Research & Policy,
DOI 10.1057/978-1-137-59010-7